Prayers That Avail Much
for Teens

Prayers That Avail Much
for Teens

by
Word Ministries

Harrison House
Tulsa, Oklahoma

5th Printing
Over 68,000 in Print
Prayers That Avail Much for Teens
ISBN 0-89274-813-3
Copyright © 1991 by Word Ministries

Published by Harrison House, Inc.
P. O. Box 35035
Tulsa, Oklahoma 74153

CONTENTS

Part III Prayers for Others

Part IV Special Prayers

FOREWORD*

The prayers in this book are to be used by you for yourself and for others. They are a matter of the heart. Deliberately feed them into your spirit. Allow the Holy Spirit to make the Word a reality in your heart. Your spirit will become quickened to God's Word, and you will begin to think like God thinks and talk like He talks. You will find yourself poring over His Word — hungering for more and more. The Father rewards those who diligently seek Him. (Heb. 11:6.)

Meditate upon the Scriptures listed with these prayers. These are by no means the only Scriptures on certain subjects, but they are a beginning.

These prayers are to be a help and a guide to you in order for you to get better acquainted with your heavenly Father and His Word. Not only does His Word affect your life, but also it will affect others through you, for you will be able to counsel accurately those who come to you for advice. If you cannot counsel someone with the Word, you do not have anything with which to counsel. Walk in God's counsel, and prize His wisdom. (Ps. 1; Prov. 4:7,8.) People are looking for something on which they can depend. When someone in need comes to you, you can point him to that portion in God's Word that is the answer to his problem. You become victorious,

---

*From *Prayers That Avail Much, Volume I*, by Word Ministries (Tulsa: Harrison House, 1989) (hereafter cited as *Prayers I*).

trustworthy, and the one with the answer, for your heart is fixed and established on His Word. (Ps. 112.)

Once you begin delving into God's Word, you must commit to ordering your conversation aright. (Ps. 50:23.) That is being a doer of the Word. Faith always has a good report. You cannot pray effectively for yourself, for someone else, or about something and then talk negatively about the matter. (Matt. 12:34-37.) This is being double-minded, and a double-minded man receives *nothing* from God. (James 1:6-8.)

In Ephesians 4:29,30 AMP it is written:

> Let no foul or polluting language, nor evil word, nor unwholesome or worthless talk [ever] come out of your mouth; but only such [speech] as is good and beneficial to the spiritual progress of others, as is fitting to the need and the occasion, that it may be a blessing and give grace (God's favor) to those who hear it.
>
> And do not grieve the Holy Spirit of God, (do not offend, or vex, or sadden Him) by whom you were sealed (marked, branded as God's own, secured) for the day of redemption — of final deliverance through Christ from evil and the consequences of sin.

Allow these words to sink into your innermost being. Our Father has much, so very much, to say about that little member, the tongue. (James 3.) Give the devil no opportunity by getting into worry, unforgiveness, strife, and criticism. Put a stop to idle and foolish talking. (Eph. 4:27; 5:4.) You are to be a blessing to others. (Gal. 6:10.)

Talk the answer, not the problem. The answer is in God's Word. You must have knowledge of that Word — revelation knowledge. (1 Cor. 2:7-16.)

As an intercessor, unite with others in prayer. United prayer is a mighty weapon that the Body of Christ is to use.

Believe you receive when you pray. Confess the Word. Hold fast to your confession of faith in God's Word. Allow your spirit to pray by the Holy Spirit. Praise God for the victory *now* before any manifestation. *Walk by faith and not by sight.* (2 Cor. 5:7.)

Don't be moved by adverse circumstances. As Satan attempts to challenge you, resist him steadfast in the faith — letting patience have her perfect work. (James 1:4.) Take the Sword of the Spirit and the shield of faith and quench his every fiery dart. (Eph. 6:16,17.) The entire substitutionary work of Christ was for you. Satan is now a defeated foe because Jesus conquered him. (Col. 2:14,15.) Satan is overcome by the blood of the Lamb and the Word of our testimony. (Rev. 12:11.) Fight the good fight of faith. (1 Tim. 6:12.) Withstand the adversary and be firm in faith against his onset — rooted, established, strong, and determined. (1 Pet. 5:9.) Speak God's Word boldly and courageously.

Your desire should be to please and to bless the Father. As you pray in line with His Word, He joyfully hears that you — His child — are living and walking in the Truth. (3 John 4.)

How exciting to know that the prayers of the saints are forever in the throne room. (Rev. 5:8.) Hallelujah!

Praise God for His Word and the limitlessness of prayer in the name of Jesus. It belongs to every child of God. Therefore, run with patience the race that is set before you, looking unto Jesus the author and finisher of your faith. (Heb. 12:1,2.) God's Word is able to build you up and give you your rightful inheritance among all God's set apart ones. (Acts 20:32.)

Commit yourself to pray and to pray correctly by approaching the throne with your mouth filled with His Word!

ACKNOWLEDGMENTS

The publisher wishes to acknowledge the following people: Kathy Brandt, Abigail Cundiff, Eugene Ichinose, Lorrie Medford, Beth Roe, and the Rhema "Fusion" youth group for their help with this book.

INTRODUCTION*

> ...The earnest (heart-felt, continued) prayer
> of a righteous man makes tremendous power
> available — dynamic in its working.
>
> James 5:16 AMP

Prayer is fellowshiping with the Father — a
vital, personal contact with God Who is more
than enough. We are to be in constant
communion with Him:

> For the eyes of the Lord are upon the
> righteous — those who are upright and in right
> standing with God — and His ears are attentive
> (open) to their prayer....
>
> 1 Peter 3:12 AMP

Prayer is not to be a religious form with no
power. It is to be effective and accurate and bring
results. God watches over His Word to perform
it. (Jer. 1:12.)

Prayer that brings results must be based on
God's Word.

> For the Word that God speaks is alive and full
> of power — making it active, operative,
> energizing and effective; it is sharper than any
> two-edged sword, penetrating to the dividing line
> of the breath of life (soul) and [the immortal]
> spirit, and of joints and marrow [that is, of the
> deepest parts of our nature] exposing and sifting
> and analyzing and judging the very thoughts and
> purposes of the heart.
>
> Hebrews 4:12 AMP

Prayer is this "living" Word in our mouths.
Our mouths must speak forth faith, for faith is

---

*From *Prayers I.*

1

what pleases God. (Heb. 11:6.) We hold His Word up to Him in prayer, and our Father sees Himself in His Word.

God's Word is our contact with Him. We put Him in remembrance of His Word (Is. 43:26) placing a demand on His ability in the name of our Lord Jesus. We remind Him that He supplies all of our needs according to His riches in glory by Christ Jesus. (Phil. 4:19.) That Word does not return to Him void — without producing any effect, useless — but it *shall* accomplish that which He pleases and purposes, and it shall prosper in the thing for which He sent it. (Is. 55:11.) Hallelujah!

God did *not* leave us without His thoughts and His ways for we have His Word — His bond. God instructs us to call Him, and He will answer and show us great and mighty things. (Jer. 33:3.) Prayer is to be exciting — not drudgery.

It takes someone to pray. God moves as we pray in faith — believing. He says that His eyes run to and fro throughout the whole earth to show Himself strong in behalf of those whose hearts are blameless toward Him. (2 Chron. 16:9.) We are blameless. (Eph. 1:4.) We are His very own children. (Eph. 1:5.) We are His righteousness in Christ Jesus. (2 Cor. 5:21.) He tells us to come boldly to the throne of grace and *obtain* mercy and find grace to help in time of need — appropriate and well-timed help. (Heb. 4:16.) Praise the Lord!

The prayer armor is for every believer, every member of the Body of Christ, who will put it on and walk in it, for the weapons of our warfare are *not carnal* but mighty through God for the

2

pulling down of the strongholds of the enemy (Satan, the god of this world, and all his demonic forces). Spiritual warfare takes place in prayer. (2 Cor. 10:4, Eph. 6:12,18.)

There are many different kinds of prayer, such as the prayer of thanksgiving and praise, the prayer of dedication and worship, and the prayer that changes *things* (not God). All prayer involves a time of fellowshipping with the Father.

In Ephesians 6, we are instructed to take the Sword of the Spirit which is the Word of God and **pray at all times — on every occasion, in every season — in the Spirit, with all [manner of] prayer and entreaty** (Eph. 6:18 AMP).

In 1 Timothy 2 we are admonished and urged that **petitions, prayers, intercessions and thanksgivings be offered on behalf of all men** (1 Tim. 2:1 AMP). *Prayer is our responsibility.*

Prayer must be the foundation of every Christian endeavor. Any failure is a prayer failure. We are *not* to be ignorant concerning God's Word. God desires for His people to be successful, to be filled with a full, deep, and clear knowledge of His will (His Word), and to bear fruit in every good work. (Col. 1:9-13.) We then bring honor and glory to Him. (John 15:8.) He desires that we know how to pray for **the prayer of the upright is his delight** (Prov. 15:8).

Our Father has not left us helpless. Not only has He given us His Word, but also He has given us the Holy Spirit to help our infirmities when we know not how to pray as we ought. (Rom. 8:26.) Praise God! Our Father has provided His people with every possible avenue to insure their

3

complete and total victory in this life in the name of our Lord Jesus. (1 John 5:3-5.)

We pray to the Father, in the name of Jesus, through the Holy Spirit, according to the Word!

Using God's Word on purpose, specifically, in prayer is one means of prayer, and it is a most effective and accurate means. Jesus said, **The words (truths) that I have been speaking to you are spirit and life** (John 6:63 AMP).

When Jesus faced Satan in the wilderness, He said, "It is written...it is written...it is written." We are to live, be upheld, and sustained by every Word that proceeds from the mouth of God. (Matt. 4:4.)

James, by the Spirit, admonishes that we do not have, because we do not ask. We ask and receive not, because we ask amiss. (James 4:2,3.) We must heed that admonishment now for we are to become experts in prayer rightly dividing the Word of Truth. (2 Tim. 2:15.)

Using the Word in prayer is *not* taking it out of context, for His Word in us is the key to answered prayer — to prayer that brings results. He is able to do exceedingly abundantly above all we ask or think, according to the power that works in us. (Eph. 3:20.) The power lies within God's Word. It is anointed by the Holy Spirit. The Spirit of God does not lead us apart from the Word, for the Word is of the Spirit of God. We apply that Word personally to ourselves and to others — not adding to or taking from it — in the name of Jesus. We apply the Word to the *now* — to those things, circumstances, and situations facing each of us *now*.

Paul was very specific and definite in his praying. The first chapters of Ephesians, Philippians, Colossians, and 2 Thessalonians are examples of how Paul prayed for believers. There are numerous others. *Search them out.* Paul wrote under the inspiration of the Holy Spirit. We can use these Spirit-given prayers today!

In 2 Corinthians 1:11, 2 Corinthians 9:14, and Philippians 1:4, we see examples of how believers prayed one for another — putting others first in their prayer life with *joy*. Our faith does work by love. (Gal. 5:6.) We grow spiritually as we reach out to help others — praying for and with them and holding out to them the Word of Life. (Phil. 2:16.)

Man is a spirit, he has a soul, and he lives in a body. (1 Thess. 5:23.) In order to operate successfully, each of these three parts must be fed properly. The soul or intellect feeds on intellectual food to produce intellectual strength. The body feeds on physical food to produce physical strength. The spirit — the heart or inward man — is the real you, the part that has been reborn in Christ Jesus. It must feed on spirit food which is God's Word in order to produce and develop faith. As we feast upon God's Word, our minds become renewed with His Word, and we have a fresh mental and spiritual attitude. (Eph. 4:23,24.)

Likewise, we are to present our bodies a living sacrifice, holy, acceptable unto God (Rom. 12:1) and not let that body dominate us but bring it into subjection to the spirit man. (1 Cor. 9:27.) God's Word is healing and health to all our flesh. (Prov. 4:22.) Therefore, God's Word affects each part of us — spirit, soul and body. We become vitally united to the Father, to Jesus, and to the Holy Spirit — one with Them. (John 16:13-15, John 17:21, Col. 2:10.)

God's Word, this spirit food, takes root in our hearts, is formed by the tongue, and is spoken out of our mouths. This is creative power. The spoken Word works as we confess it and then apply the action to it.

Be doers of the Word, and not hearers only, deceiving your own selves. (James 1:22.) Faith without works or corresponding action is *dead*. (James 2:17.) Don't be mental assenters — those who agree that the Bible is true but never act on it. *Real faith is acting on God's Word now.* We cannot build faith without practicing the Word. We cannot develop an effective prayer life that is anything but empty words unless God's Word actually has a part in our lives. We are to hold fast to our *confession* of the Word's truthfulness. Our Lord Jesus is the High Priest of our confession (Heb. 3:1), and He is the Guarantee of a better agreement — a more excellent and advantageous covenant. (Heb. 7:22.)

Prayer does not cause faith to work, but faith causes prayer to work. Therefore, any prayer problem is a problem of doubt — doubting the integrity of the Word and the ability of God to stand behind His promises or the statements of fact in the Word.

We can spend fruitless hours in prayer if our hearts are not prepared beforehand. Preparation of the heart, the spirit, comes from meditation in the Father's Word, meditation on who we are in Christ, what He is to us, and what the Holy

6

Spirit can mean to us as we become God-inside minded. As God told Joshua (Josh. 1:8), as we meditate on the Word day and night, and do according to all that is written, then shall we make our way prosperous and have good success. We are to attend to God's Word, submit to His sayings, keep them in the center of our hearts, and put away contrary talk. (Prov. 4:20-24.)

When we use God's Word in prayer, this is *not* something we just rush through uttering once, and we are finished. Do *not* be mistaken. There is nothing "magical" nor "manipulative" about it — no set pattern or device in order to satisfy what we want or think out of our flesh. Instead we are holding God's Word before Him. We confess what He says belongs to us.

We expect His divine intervention while we choose not to look at the things that are seen but at the things that are unseen, for the things that are seen are subject to change. (2 Cor. 4:18.)

Prayer based upon the Word rises above the senses, contacts the Author of the Word and sets His spiritual laws into motion. It is not just saying prayers that gets results, but it is spending time with the Father, learning His wisdom, drawing on His strength, being filled with His quietness, and basking in His love that bring results to our prayers. Praise the Lord!

* * *

The prayers in this book are designed to teach and train you in the art of personal confession and intercessory prayer. As you pray them, you will be reinforcing the prayer armor which we have been instructed to put on in Ephesians 6:11. The fabric from which the armor is made is the Word of God. We are to live by every word that proceeds from the mouth of God. We desire the whole counsel of God, because we know it changes us. By receiving that counsel, you will be ... **transformed (changed) by the [entire] renewal of your mind — by its new ideals and attitude — so that you may prove [for yourselves] what is the good and acceptable and perfect will of God, even the thing which is good and acceptable and perfect [in His sight for you]** (Rom. 12:2 AMP).

The prayers of personal confession of the Word of God for yourself can also be used as intercessory prayers for others by simply praying them in the third person, changing the pronouns *I* or *we* to the name of the person or persons for whom you are interceding and adjusting the verbs accordingly.

The prayers of intercession have blanks in which you (individually or as a group) are to fill in the spaces with the name of the person(s) for whom you are praying. These prayers of intercession can likewise be made into prayers of personal confession for yourself (or your group) by inserting your own name(s) and the proper personal pronouns in the appropriate places.

An often-asked question is: "How many times should I pray the same prayer?"

The answer is simple: you pray until you know that the answer is fixed in your heart. After that, you need to repeat the prayer whenever adverse circumstances or long delays cause you to be tempted to doubt that your prayer has been heard and your request granted.

The Word of God is your weapon against the temptation to lose heart and grow weary in your prayer life. When that Word of promise becomes fixed in your heart, you will find yourself praising, giving glory to God for the answer, even when the only evidence you have of that answer is your own faith.

Another question often asked is: "When we repeat prayers more than once, aren't we praying 'vain repetitions'?"

Obviously, such people are referring to the admonition of Jesus when He told His disciples: **And when you pray do not (multiply words, repeating the same ones over and over, and) heap up phrases as the Gentiles do, for they think they will be heard for their much speaking** (Matt. 6:7 AMP). Praying the Word of God is not praying the kind of prayer that the "heathen" pray. You will note in 1 Kings 18:25-29 the manner of prayer that was offered to the gods who could not hear. That is not the way you and I pray. The words that we speak are not vain, but they are spirit and life, and mighty through God to the pulling down of strongholds. We have a God Whose eyes are over the righteous and Whose ears are open to us: when we pray, He hears us.

You are the righteousness of God in Christ Jesus, and your prayers will avail much. They will bring salvation to the sinner, deliverance to the oppressed, healing to the sick, and prosperity to the poor. They will usher in the next move of God in the earth. In addition to affecting outward

9

circumstances and other people, your prayers will also have an effect upon you. In the very process of praying, your life will be changed as you go from faith to faith and from glory to glory.

As a Christian, your first priority is to love the Lord your God with your entire being, and your neighbor as yourself. You are called to be an intercessor, a man or woman of prayer. You are to seek the face of the Lord as you inquire, listen, meditate and consider in the temple of the Lord.

As one of "God's set-apart ones," the will of the Lord for your life is the same as it is for the life of every other true believer: **...seek ye first the kingdom of God, and his righteousness; and all these things shall be added unto you** (Matt. 6:33).

PERSONAL CONFESSIONS*

Jesus is Lord over my spirit, my soul, and my body. (Phil. 2:9-11.)

Jesus has been made unto me wisdom, righteousness, sanctification, and redemption. I can do all things through Christ Who strengthens me. (1 Cor. 1:30, Phil. 4:13.)

The Lord is my shepherd. I do not want. My God supplies all my need according to His riches in glory in Christ Jesus. (Ps. 23, Phil. 4:19.)

I do not fret or have anxiety about anything. I do not have a care. (Phil. 4:6, 1 Pet. 5:6,7.)

I am the Body of Christ. I am redeemed from the curse, because Jesus bore my sicknesses and carried my diseases in His own body. By His stripes I am healed. I forbid any sickness or disease to operate in my body. Every organ, every tissue of my body functions in the perfection in which God created it to function. I honor God and bring glory to Him in my body. (Gal. 3:13, Matt. 8:17, 1 Pet. 2:24, 1 Cor. 6:20.)

I have the mind of Christ and hold the thoughts, feelings, and purposes of His heart. (1 Cor. 2:16.)

I am a believer and not a doubter. I hold fast to my confession of faith. I decide to walk by faith and practice faith. My faith comes by hearing and hearing by the Word of God. Jesus is the author

---

*From *Prayers I*.

and the developer of my faith. (Heb. 4:14, Heb. 11:6, Rom. 10:17, Heb. 12:2.)

The love of God has been shed abroad in my heart by the Holy Spirit and His love abides in me richly. I keep myself in the Kingdom of light, in love, in the Word, and the wicked one touches me not. (Rom. 5:5, 1 John 4:16, 1 John 5:18.)

I tread upon serpents and scorpions and over all the power of the enemy. I take my shield of faith and quench his every fiery dart. Greater is He Who is in me than he who is in the world. (Ps. 91:13, Eph. 6:16, 1 John 4:4.)

I am delivered from this present evil world. I am seated with Christ in heavenly places. I reside in the Kingdom of God's dear Son. The law of the Spirit of life in Christ Jesus has made me free from the law of sin and death. (Gal. 1:4, Eph. 2:6, Col. 1:13, Rom. 8:2.)

I fear *not* for God has given me a spirit of power, of love, and of a sound mind. God is on my side. (2 Tim. 1:7, Rom. 8:31.)

I hear the voice of the Good Shepherd. I hear my Father's voice, and the voice of a stranger I will not follow. I roll my works upon the Lord. I commit and trust them wholly to Him. He will cause my thoughts to become agreeable to His will, and so shall my plans be established and succeed. (John 10:27, Prov. 16:3.)

I am a world overcomer because I am born of God. I represent the Father and Jesus well. I am a useful member in the Body of Christ. I am His workmanship recreated in Christ Jesus. My Father God is all the while effectually at work in me both to will and do His good pleasure. (1 John 5:4,5, Eph. 2:10, Phil. 2:13.)

I let the Word dwell in me richly. He Who began a good work in me will continue until the day of Christ. (Col. 3:16, Phil. 1:6.)

Part I

DAILY PRAYERS

— 1 —

COMMITMENT TO THE LORD

Father, I pray that Your plan for my life will be accomplished. So I submit my own dreams and plans to You, and make sure that they line up with Your will for me.

Nothing on earth is as important as knowing and obeying You. My relationship with You is my number one priority. So I concentrate on Your will and Your Word, not on people's opinions and ideas or on temporary circumstances. I'll not be moved by what I feel or see; I'll only be moved by what I believe. And I believe You above all else.

Father, You are awesome and incredible. Please help me to keep the fire burning in my heart to live my life fully sold out to You. I have to have You in first place in my life, so I determine to hunger and thirst for Your Word and Your will for me. And I know that You will satisfy this desire because You promised me in Your Word that when I look for You with all my heart, then I will find You. I'm going to look for You even more, Father, in Your Word and in prayer. Teach me to do Your will so that I can always please You and do the good works that You have planned for me to do.

I choose to love You and to love people, because I know this is Your will. I don't have to wait until I am older to dedicate my heart to You.

17

So I commit and dedicate my whole body, mind, and spirit to You in Jesus' name.

You are my life and I will obey and love You every day. I realize that I am not my own, but that You bought me back from the devil with the price of Jesus' blood. Satan doesn't own any part of me anymore and he has no authority in my life. So help me not to follow even one step of the way in which Satan leads.

I serve Jesus and keep His commandments; I will not follow the voice of a stranger. So I separate myself from ungodly people and determine to live holy, just as You are holy, Father. I'll talk and act as I would if I could physically see You standing next to me, because I know that You are always with me and in me. Thank You that You chose me — actually picked me out for Yourself as Your own child — that I should be holy and blameless in Your sight.

I decide to follow You as long as I live. I trust You to lead me and guide me through Your Word and by the Holy Spirit. Please teach me to follow and imitate You, Father, just as children imitate their parents.

In Jesus' name I want to always move forward. This isn't the time to grow slack or the place to turn back. I'll never go back to the "Egypt" of sin, deception, and death. Not my will, but Yours be done, Father.

In Jesus' name I pray. Amen.

Scripture References

Colossians 2:20-22
Colossians 3:1-3
Psalm 42:1
Matthew 5:6 AMP
Jeremiah 29:13
Psalm 91:14

Luke 10:27
Jeremiah 42:6
Psalm 37:4,5
Lamentations 3:25
Acts 17:24,27,28
Colossians 1:9

— 2 —

PRAISE AND THANKSGIVING

Father, I love You and praise You. You're such a wonderful God. You deserve thanks and praise because You are so great and Your love endures forever. I'll praise You all day and all night. I'll continually thank You for being so good and merciful to me. You alone are worthy of praise, thanksgiving, glory, honor, power and dominion.

I won't forget that You've given me so many good things like good health and everlasting life with You in heaven. Thank You for sending Jesus to die for me and to remove my sins as far from me as the east is from the west. Jesus won the victory for me and made me clean and right in Your eyes. Thank You so much! Alleluia!

You are so loving, kind, and slow to anger. You're my strength and my joy. I'll sing about all the good things that You've done for me. People will know that I'm a Christian by my love, hope, and happiness.

Father, You created the heavens, the earth, the sea, and everything in them. Thank You for making me so I can enjoy life to the fullest. You made this day for me to be glad in it and enjoy it.

Because You are always with me, nothing can stand against me. I will not be afraid of anything because You will never leave me or reject me. Father, You are 100 percent totally good. Nothing evil like sickness, death, or poverty comes from You. You give only good and perfect gifts.

I thank You and praise You for supplying and providing everything I need. You are all-powerful, You know everything, and You are everywhere. Thank You for being such a loving Father to me and giving Jesus to be my Savior, Lord, and Friend. Thank You for sending the Holy Spirit to fill me, guide me, comfort me, and teach me the right things to do.

I'll always praise You, in every good day, in every bad day, in every sunny day, and even in the dark days. I'm going to sing from my heart so I can have the words to show the world how I feel about my awesome God. No matter what happens, I'll praise You now and as long as I live. Even if I don't feel like it, I'm going to give You praise and glory because You've been so generous to me.

In Jesus' name I pray. Amen.

Scripture References

Psalm 48:1	Psalm 103:2
Psalm 71:8	Psalm 103:8
Psalm 34:1	Psalm 18:30
Psalm 136:1	Revelation 4:8,11
Psalm 63:3,4,5 NIV	John 10:10
Psalm 28:7	

— 3 —

WISDOM AND GOD'S WILL

Heavenly Father, I am making a special request that I may be filled with the clear knowledge of Your will in all wisdom and understanding. I don't need to follow my own will or anybody else's will, but I need to follow after Your will. I know that Your will and Your Word agree, so I'll continue to stay in Your Word and meditate on it every day, so that I can know Your plan and Your purpose for this season in my life. I want to live in a way that is worthy of You and fully pleasing to You, not just partially, but fully bringing You pleasure.

I roll all my cares and works on to You. As I follow after Your Word and stay in prayer, I believe You will cause my thoughts to agree with Yours, so that I may be fruitful in every good work.

You have said that Your wisdom is pure and full of compassion. So I ask You that my love and compassion may grow to their fullest development so I can be strong in faith and love, and pure and blameless before You, not stumbling nor causing others to stumble. For as I grow in love, I grow in You. As I grow in You, I grow in the knowledge of Your will and Your wisdom.

So help me to become more like Jesus. Help me to feed on Your Word. For wisdom and understanding come from Your mouth. Please teach me to meditate on Your Word. For Your words contain a wealth of wisdom that makes me wiser than all of my teachers.

As for this situation today, I thank You for Your wisdom in knowing the right thing to do and to say. I give my ear to You, and decide to listen to You. Teach me the way that You want me to go. Thank You for counseling me and watching over me carefully. Thank You for the Holy Spirit on the inside of me; He's my Teacher and Guide. I believe He's active in my life, now.

I know because I read in Your Word that the Holy Spirit will tell me the right thing to do. I won't be afraid or confused because Your Word brings me light and understanding. Although there are many voices in the world, I'll follow the voice of my Shepherd. The voice of a stranger I will not follow.

Thank You for the wise parents, teachers, and pastors You've put in my life. They are people whom You can use to teach and instruct me. So I will seek counsel from them on major decisions and changes. When I need to make an important, final decision, I'm always going to follow the peace that comes from knowing Your will, Father. I may have plans in my mind, but Your plans will be the most important, and You can determine which way in life that I'm supposed to go.

I dedicate everything that I do to You, and because of that, I know that my plans will succeed. I will trust You with my life and everything in it, more than I have ever trusted anyone else before. I thank You that as I follow after You, I can follow after peace in my heart. I thank You for Your wisdom.

In Jesus' name I pray. Amen.

Scripture References

James 1:5,6
Proverbs 2:6
Colossians 1:9
Ephesians 5:15
Colossians 3:16
Psalm 32:8
Psalm 16:7
Joshua 1:9
1 Corinthians 14:33 KJV

Psalm 119:99
Proverbs 6:20-23
Proverbs 19:21
Psalm 119:130,133
Proverbs 16:9
Proverbs 16:3
Psalm 118:8
James 3:17

— 4 —

PRIORITIES

Father, I need Your help to set my priorities in the right order. First, please help me to love You with all of my heart, mind, and body, and to love others the way You do.

Your Word says that when I put You first, by making You number one in my life, then everything else that I need and desire will be given to me. Thank You for helping me to put You first by reading Your Word, and talking to You in prayer every day.

Father, after my relationship with You and Jesus, my next priority is my family. Please help me to obey my parents and to love and cherish my family, because I know this is important to You. With Your help I can walk in love even when I'm tempted to get mad, or rebel, or get into arguments with them.

After my family, please help me to put school, work, and church in the right perspective. I desire to be faithful, diligent, disciplined, and consistent with all of my work at school, on my job, and at church.

I desire to do all of my activities and work for You, and not to impress people. I know You will reward me even if people sometimes don't give me the credit I deserve. When I put You first, I can be successful at whatever I do.

Finally, Father, help me to put my relationship with friends — and all my other activities like ball games, parties, road trips, and dates — in the right priority. I don't want to major on minor things. I want to major on the things that are important to You. Thank You for showing me the priorities that will make the difference in my life. Help me to do ordinary things extraordinarily well.

I know that Jesus came that I might have life, and have it to the fullest. I know You want me to have a good time by meeting people, laughing, and doing fun things. I believe that by putting You first and by keeping all my priorities in the right order I will be closer to You and have a great church, school, work, and social life.

By faith I believe I can have more fun, excitement, adventure, laughs, good times, and close friends by following You than I could have by following the devil down his path to death and destruction while enjoying the pleasure of sin for a short season.

Thank You, Father, for helping me to set my priorities in the right order.

In Jesus' name I pray. Amen.

Scripture References

Luke 10:27	Psalm 1:2,3
Matthew 6:33	Joshua 1:7,8
Proverbs 4:7,8	Proverbs 3:5,6
Colossians 1:16	Psalm 37:4

— 5 —

PROTECTION

Father God, Your Word says that if I will stay close to You in prayer and in my relationship with You, then I will be safe and protected from all evil and injury. You are my stronghold and my fortress. You are my God; in You will I trust. Surely You will deliver me from the devil's traps and schemes to hurt me. I will not be afraid of any terror at night, nor of any evil or wicked person during the day.

Lord, faith in Your Word is a shield to protect me from all the fiery darts of the Evil One. Because You are for me, no one can stand against me. Although I walk through the valley of the shadow of death, I will fear no evil because You are always with me. Even during a terrible storm I can have peace in my heart because perfect love casts out all fear. You have not given me a spirit of fear, but of power and of love and of a sound mind.

Your Word promises that no evil will come upon me, no accident will overtake me, and no disease or tragedy will come near my home. Thank You for giving Your angels the command to keep me safe in all that I do. They will surround me and lift me up in their hands so I'll always be safe.

Because I have set my love upon You, therefore You will deliver me and protect me from trouble and satisfy me with a long life. When I call upon You, You always answer me, and when I'm in trouble You're always with me.

I know that You're in me and that You're greater than the devil or any evil person in the world. And You promised me that no weapon aimed at me will succeed. So I'll be strong, courageous, and fearless.

Father, You promised Your children a sweet, peaceful sleep, so thank You that I can rest at night free from fear or nightmares. You give me peace and rest; Jesus is my safety. Thank You for protecting me.

In Jesus' name I pray. Amen.

To remind yourself of God's protection, read Psalm 91 and Psalm 23 often.

Scripture References

Psalm 34:7 AMP	Joshua 1:8
Psalm 91	Deuteronomy 7:9
John 10:10	Daniel 6:22
1 John 3:8	2 Kings 6:17
Psalm 4:8	Psalm 23

— 6 —

HEALING

Father, Your Word says that whatever I ask for in prayer, if I believe I've received it, it will be mine. So I come to Your throne boldly by faith to receive healing of _____.

Thank You that Jesus took my sicknesses, carried away my diseases, and provided healing for me 2,000 years ago. Healing isn't something You might do, or could do, or would do if I were good enough; healing is something that You've already done for me. Because of the stripes on Jesus' back, I believe that I am healed now. Sickness is under the curse of the law, and Jesus saved me from the curse; so that means that Jesus saved me from this sickness.

I know that the reason You sent Jesus and anointed Him with the Holy Spirit and power was so He could loose mankind and set us free from all the works of the devil. Jesus provided healing for all who are oppressed by sickness and disease. Jesus is the same today as He was yesterday and will be tomorrow; He never varies nor even has a shadow of change. Because Jesus healed in Bible days, I know it's His will to heal me today, right now.

Jesus saved me from the curse of sickness by dying on the cross and rising from the dead. He took my sicknesses and diseases, so I wouldn't have to bear them. Because You are the God Who heals me, I refuse to let this sickness stay in my body. I won't tolerate it. Satan has to take his hands off of me because I am God's property. I have on the whole armor of God, and the shield of faith protects me from all the fiery darts of the devil.

Healing is the children's bread and I'm Your child, so I receive total and complete healing for my body and mind, from the top of my head to the soles of my feet. You've given me Your Word on it, and that's good enough for me.

I believe that I'm beginning to get better right now, from this very moment. I may or may not feel better right away, but my faith is not based on what I feel, or what I see; it's based on Jesus, the Word of God. If Jesus said it, I believe it. His Word never lies. If it's written in the Bible, I'll believe it until I die. Though the mountains be removed and cast into the sea, I'll believe Your Word throughout eternity. Nothing is too hard or impossible for You.

Your Word is health, life, and medicine to my whole body. I speak what's in my heart, so I will put Your Word in my heart every day. Father, Your Word says that my tongue has the power of life and death, so please help me to speak over my body only words filled with faith, hope, life and health. I will not let any words of sickness, death, or unbelief cross my lips.

Faith works because of love, so I won't have any unforgiveness, bitterness, or sin in my life. I ask the Holy Spirit, the Great Comforter, to comfort my pains and hurts so I will have a sweet and peaceful sleep tonight.

Because faith calls those things that be not as though they were, I call myself healed. Father, thank You for healing me.

In Jesus' name I pray. Amen.

Once this has been prayed, thank the Father that Satan is bound and continue to confess this healing, thanking God for it.

Scripture References

Exodus 15:26

1 Peter 2:24

Acts 10:38 KJV

Hebrews 13:8

1 John 3:8

Luke 10:19

Matthew 18:18

Mark 16:17,18

1 Corinthians 11:23-25 NIV

Psalm 91:2

1 Corinthians 11:25

Galatians 3:13

Psalm 103:3

John 10:10

Mark 1:23,24

John 14:14

Proverbs 4:20-22

Proverbs 18:21

Isaiah 53:5

Deuteronomy 28

FINANCES

Father, thank You for being my source of total supply. Everything that is good comes from You — either directly or indirectly — so I look to You as my source of finances.

Before I even ask, You know that I need money to give my tithes and offerings, for clothes, transportation, school, and entertainment. You said that the things I desire will be given to me if I will ask You for them and really believe in faith that You will give them to me. Because I trust You, I ask specifically for $_____ to meet my financial needs.

I know that You can use many instruments, such as jobs and parents, to bless me financially, and I will cherish and respect those instruments; but I still recognize You as my main source. When one instrument dries up or is cut off, I won't worry, because I still have You to provide for my every financial need. Your Word says that You take pleasure in the prosperity of Your servant.

Because You have given me the ability to make money, I'll look for good ideas and opportunities to earn the money that I need. If I keep a good attitude and work hard, You will help me to be very successful. You will give me favor with people so they'll want to help me.

Father, You made the heavens and the earth, and You own the silver, the gold, and all the cattle on a thousand hills. So my financial need is a small thing to You because nothing is too hard or impossible for You. I thank You that Your angels are working for me to help bring in the finances that I need.

Your Word promises that if I give my tithes and offerings to You cheerfully, without complaining, I will always have enough. Because I am a tither (giving 10 percent of all my income back to God), there is a special protection over my finances and You can stretch my money and cause it to go further. I know that what I have given to You will be given back to me and even more than I can receive.

I won't put You in a box by trying to figure out exactly where the money will come from — that's not my business — but my part is to stay in faith and to be very grateful and thankful to You and to the people You use to meet my needs. Because I am Your child, I believe You will bless those who bless me.

And please help me to handle my money wisely by always putting a portion of my income into savings and by being a generous giver so that I won't get into financial crunches all of the time. Like a farmer, I'll always be planting seed so I can always be reaping a harvest.

Thank You for meeting my financial needs and wanting me to prosper, and enjoy life to the fullest.

In Jesus' name I pray. Amen.

Scripture References

Matthew 6:33	Deuteronomy 8:18
Psalm 34:10	Proverbs 3:9,10
Isaiah 65:24	2 Corinthians 9:7
Numbers 23:19	Malachi 3:10,11 KJV
Proverbs 3:4	Luke 6:38
James 1:17	Deuteronomy 28:1-13
Philippians 4:19 NIV	Proverbs 10:4
Psalm 23:1	Genesis 12:2,3
Psalm 89:11	Ecclesiastes 5:19
Haggai 2:8	Psalm 35:27

— 8 —

CONTROLLING YOUR THOUGHTS/RENEWING YOUR MIND

Father, You know all of my thoughts and the attitudes of my heart. Help me make my thoughts and words pleasing to You. I can do this because You have not given me a spirit of fear, but of power, and of love, and of a sound mind.

With Your help I'll control my thoughts and cast down any thought of fear, hate, lust, envy, jealousy, or selfishness. You gave me Your Word as a weapon to fight impure and unholy thoughts. Your Word is alive and more powerful than any weapon known to man, and it pulls down the strongholds that Satan tries to build in my mind.

I realize that my mind doesn't stay renewed any more than my hair stays combed, so I will continue to renew and clean my mind by washing it with the water of Your Word to clean out any bad or evil thought. I will not allow fear or worry to dominate my thinking. I now choose to concentrate on things that are pure, holy, true, right, and clean. I choose to think godly thoughts rather than thinking the thoughts that sinners think.

Bad thoughts are like birds; I can't keep them from flying over my head, but I can sure keep them from making a nest in my hair. So I refuse to dwell on negative or impure thoughts. When a bad thought flashes across my mind, like a picture on a TV screen, I'll just change the channel by speaking the Word of God.

I thank You for giving me the helmet of salvation to guard my thoughts. As I commit to stay in Your Word daily, I will begin to think more and more like You, Father. I will diligently guard my mind and heart by not watching or reading anything that will pollute my thinking.

Thank You for giving me the mind of Christ. Help me to make all my thoughts obedient to Jesus, the Word.

In Jesus' name I pray. Amen.

Scripture References

Psalm 139:2-4	Psalm 139:23
Psalm 94:11	Philippians 4:6-8 NIV
Isaiah 55:8,9	Colossians 3:2
2 Corinthians 10:3-5 KJV	Isaiah 26:3 KJV
Psalm 19:14 NIV	Proverbs 16:3 KJV
1 Corinthians 2:16	Proverbs 3:26
Hebrews 4:12	Psalm 138:8 KJV

— 9 —

CONTROLLING WHAT YOU SAY

Father, Your Word says in Proverbs 17:27,28 (AMP), **He who has knowledge spares his words, and a man of understanding has a cool spirit. Even a fool when he holds his peace is considered wise; when he closes his lips he is esteemed a man of understanding.** Proverbs 29:20 (KJV) also says, **Seest thou a man that is hasty in his words? there is more hope of a fool than of him.** And James 3:2 (KJV) says, **For in many things we offend all. If any man offend not in word, the same is a perfect man, and able also to bridle the whole body.**

Lord, You said that life and death are in the power of the tongue, and that I will be satisfied by the fruit of my lips. Out of the abundance of my heart, my mouth speaks. What I think about, I talk about, and what I talk about, I bring about. I won't fill my heart with worldly things, but I'll feed my spirit on Your Word so that Your Word will be in abundance in me. Your words are life to those who find them and health to all their flesh.

When I speak Your Word, Father, it produces life and health in me. Because Jesus is the Word, the better I get to know the Bible, the better I get to know Jesus. The more I spend time with Jesus, the Word, the more I'll begin to speak faith-filled words as He does.

I believe that I can control what I say because no temptations come to me that are unique or new. You are faithful and You will make a way of escape when I am tempted to sin with my mouth. Thank You, Father, for that escape. Your Word says that truthful words will last forever, but that lying words will be exposed. Careless words spoken by gossipers or backbiters stab like a knife, but wise words bring healing. I won't say just anything that comes to my mind, but I'll think before I open my mouth. I'll be quick to hear and slow to speak.

Words are like containers. Jesus said that I would be judged for all empty and idle words. Either I can fill words with love, faith, and hope, or I can fill them with doubt, unbelief, and hate. So I choose to speak Your Word, Father — words of life, peace, joy, and faith.

Because I know that good words are sweet to hear and they bring life to people, help me always to be someone who says good things. I want to say the same things that I would say if I were holding Jesus by the hand and looking Him right in the eye.

Thank You, Father, for a pure heart and pure words.

In Jesus' name I pray. Amen.

Scripture References

Proverbs 18:21   Proverbs 10:19
Ephesians 4:29   1 Peter 5:8,9
Ephesians 4:25   James 4:7
James 4:11   1 Corinthians 10:13
Proverbs 17:9

Part II

PERSONAL PRAYERS

— 10 —

SALVATION

God, I realize that I need Jesus Christ in my life. Thank You that You love me and accept me the way I am, right now. Although You hate and despise sin, You love sinners so much that You sent Your only Son, Jesus, to pay the price that I owed. God, You are not mocked — whatever I do (or sow), that will I also reap.

The Bible says that all men have sinned and fallen short of the glory of God. I know that in my own life I have fallen way short of Your plan for me. Although the wages of sin are death, I receive salvation and eternal life as a free gift from You. I can do nothing to earn it.

I confess that I am a sinner, but I want to turn from serving myself, sin, and the devil. So I turn to Jesus and decide to walk in the light and determine in my heart that I'll never return to the darkness of sin and deception again.

God, Your Word says that whoever will call on the name of Jesus will be saved. I call on Jesus' name right now. I say out loud with my mouth that Jesus is my Lord, and I believe in my heart that God, You raised Him from the dead. I accept Your forgiveness and cleansing from all my sin. I receive the free gift of eternal life right now. I now invite You to come into my heart and life. I want to trust Jesus as Savior and follow Him as Lord.

I am no longer a child of the devil, but now I am a child of God. Help me to understand that I am saved because of faith, not because of any good deeds or emotions. I have been made a new person because of Your Son, Jesus.

I thank You that You are now my Father. I thank You for this free gift of eternal life. I thank You that my sin and iniquities You will remember no more, and You have removed my sins as far from me as the east is from the west. I am a new creation in Christ Jesus. Old things are passed away; behold, all things are become new. I have been born of the incorruptible seed of the Word of God. I have been delivered from the power of darkness and transferred into the kingdom of Your Son, Jesus. I no longer have to walk in darkness; I now can walk in the light.

Father, thank You for sending Jesus as my Savior, and making me born again.

In Jesus' name I pray. Amen.

Scripture References

Romans 3:23   Romans 10:9,10
Romans 6:23   Acts 2:38
Romans 10:13   Ephesians 2:8,9
1 John 1:9   Psalm 103:12

— 11 —

INFILLING OF THE HOLY SPIRIT

Father, I thank You that You have made it possible for me to have power in my Christian walk. You have sent the Holy Spirit as a Comforter, so that I can have power to witness and live a successful life.

I have been born again and saved. I am Your child; therefore, I am qualified to receive the Holy Spirit because I know Jesus as my Lord and Savior.

I understand that although the Holy Spirit gives me the words and phrases, I am responsible for speaking and allowing the Holy Spirit to give me my heavenly prayer language. Thank You that this prayer language is evidence that I have received the infilling of the Holy Spirit, because the Holy Spirit gives me the words to speak.

Father, when I speak in my heavenly prayer language, I am not speaking to men, but to You. Even though my mind does not understand what I am saying, my spirit does — and so do You. I know that I can pray with my prayer language as an act of my will. I thank You that praying in the Holy Spirit strengthens me and encourages my faith in You, and that I can pray mysteries in the Holy Ghost concerning my life and Your plan for me.

Your Word says that as our heavenly Father, You give the Holy Spirit to those who ask. So I ask You for the gift of the Holy Spirit. I receive Him now by faith. Thank You for filling me with the power of the Holy Ghost. I will yield myself to Him and begin to speak with other tongues. (Raise your hands toward heaven.)

In Jesus' name I praise You, Father. Alleluia! You alone are worthy of praise, thanksgiving, glory, honor, power, and dominion. I thank You, Father, for the gift of the Holy Spirit.

In Jesus' name I pray. Amen. (Yield to the Holy Spirit and begin to speak in a new tongue.)

Scripture References

Acts 1:8	1 Corinthians 14:2
John 14:16,17	Acts 2:4
Luke 11:9-13	1 Corinthians 14:15
1 John 5:14,15	Jude 20

— 12 —

FOR FAVOR WITH PARENTS, TEACHERS, FRIENDS, CO-WORKERS OR EMPLOYERS

Father, You said what things I desire when I pray that I should believe that I receive them and that I would have them. So I ask You for favor with You and with all men. Thank You that Your Word says that You give blessing to the righteous and surround them with Your favor like a shield. I am one of Your righteous children and I accept this promise for me.

I am so thankful that even when it looks as though I have no favor or backing, You have the answer.

Father, I am committed to being a doer of Your Word, and doing what I need to do in order to have Your favor. Help me to walk in love, to be merciful and kind. Help me to walk in truth every day and to control my tongue so that I speak words that build people up and not words of gossip or complaining. So many people say stupid things. I determine to speak good words.

Your Word says that if I keep Your Word and lock it in my heart, I will win favor and respect from You and from men and women, boys and girls. I thank You that I have favor with my parents, friends, classmates, teachers, co-workers, and my boss. This favor is undeserved;

45

it doesn't come by working for it or by trying to "earn it" from people. It comes only by walking closely with You, by spending time in Your Word and prayer.

I thank You that I have favor with _____ _____. I am glad that he/she has seen Your favor for me, and thank You for moving on _____'s heart on my behalf. And I ask that even if _____ may not like me right now, please turn his/her heart toward me that I might find favor in his/her eyes and so that our relationship might be improved.

Thank You for the favor that understanding and wisdom will bring to me. Every good gift is from You, so thank You that every promotion also comes from You and not from man or man's efforts. Help me to work with You and walk in Your ways, so that the opportunity to be promoted may come to me. Your Word says that when I please You, You will make my enemies friendly toward me. As I treat others with favor, mercy, love, and forgiveness, I expect that I will receive these things in return.

Thank You for hearing me and answering me, and thank You for the improvements in my relationships with my friends, family, teachers, co-workers, classmates, and employers. I am expecting good things, Father.

In Jesus' name I pray. Amen.

Scripture References

Psalm 5:12   James 1:17
Proverbs 3:1-4   Psalm 75:6,7
Proverbs 13:15   Galatians 6:7
Proverbs 8:35   Proverbs 16:7
Daniel 1:9

— 13 —

YOUR APPEARANCE

Father, I thank You for making me and for giving me life. Your Word says that You created me in Your likeness and in Your image. It also says that everything You made was good, so I thank You that You created me "good." You didn't mess up when You made me. You formed me and fashioned me and crafted me when I was in my mother's womb. I know that Jesus came so that I could enjoy life to its fullest, but that Satan came to try to steal, kill, and destroy that life.

Because Jesus destroyed all the works of the devil, I speak Your Word of life to my body, and I won't let Satan destroy any part of me. I determine to spend more time making my inward person beautiful than I do on my outward appearance. I do this by spending time with You in Your Word and in prayer, and developing a quiet and meek spirit.

I know that my outward appearance is important to You also, Father. For You care about every area of my life, and You give me the desires of my heart when I follow after You. I desire to have a body and appearance that I feel good about, that will give me confidence, and that will be nothing that I should be embarrassed about or ashamed of.

So I thank You, Father, by faith, for a good, healthy body. Please teach me to take care of myself, and to maximize all that You gave me when You created me. Teach me how to wear my hair so that it looks its best, how to choose colors and styles that look good on me, and how to take care of my skin.

Help me to listen to the Holy Spirit, the Teacher on the inside of me, keeping in mind that my body is His temple. I know there are some things, like my eye color, that I can't change, but the proportions and weight of my body can be shaped like clay. I am the clay; thank You that You are the potter.

Paul said that he kept his body under control and under subjection, and he didn't let his body do or eat just anything it wanted to. He disciplined his flesh, so I will control and discipline my body. I believe that with Your help, I can lose weight, or add and tone muscles to maximize the physical beauty of the body that You gave me.

Father, help me to exercise consistently and to take care of this temple of the Holy Spirit. Help me to be patient and to change any lifestyle or eating habits that might be destructive. I ask that You make me look the way that You intended for me to look. It may take some time, because I'm not even through growing or changing yet. So I'll continually feed on the Word of God, for it is life to me and health to all my flesh. I realize that physical beauty is not the most important issue, but it should not be neglected either.

Your Word says that You beautify the meek with salvation, so I thank You for the beauty of a godly character. I treat my body with respect because Your Holy Spirit lives in me. I know that physical appearance isn't the most important thing, so I won't become vain because of good looks or depressed because of bad looks, according to the world's standards. Help me not to be always comparing myself to others, whether they look better or worse than me. But I praise You because You are my Maker. I don't base my worth on how I look. I'm worthy because You said that I am, and that You made me that way.

I'm so valuable that You gave Your only Son so that You could buy me back from the devil. I believe that You are still working on me, perfecting everything that involves me, including the way I look. So I won't slouch; I'll stand and sit up straight, look people in the eye, and just know that You are making me look the way You want me to look.

Father, thank You for beautifying me with salvation.

In Jesus' name I pray. Amen.

Scripture References

Genesis 1:27	Proverbs 4:20-22
Genesis 1:31	1 Corinthians 6:19
Isaiah 44:2	Proverbs 31:30
John 10:10	Romans 8:17
1 Peter 2:24	Psalm 149:4

— 14 —

MEETING NEW FRIENDS

Father, I come boldly to Your throne to ask You to help me to meet some new friends. I know that You are my source of love and friendship, but You desire to express Your love and friendship toward me through other people. So I am convinced that it is Your will for me to have godly friendships with boys and girls.

Your Word reveals the purpose and value of healthy friendship. It is not the quantity but the quality of friends that matters. In Proverbs, it says that iron sharpens iron, so one friend sharpens another friend. You also said that whoever has too many friends can be setting himself up for a problem, because he may turn into a men-pleaser instead of a God-pleaser.

Father, You have said that one can chase a 1,000 and two can put 10,000 to flight. So I know that there is power in agreement. So being friendless can be a disadvantage. I know that You want the best for me, so I pray that I'll be led by Your Spirit to choose the best friends for me. All good friendships are from You so I am not going to let go of those friendships that I already have, but rather I'm going to protect them and cherish them. Your Word says that two are better than one, because if one falls, there will be someone to lift him or her up.

Of course, the greatest example of friendship is found in Jesus. He is a friend Who sticks closer than a brother. He defined the standard when He said in John 15:13 (KJV), **Greater love hath no**

man than this, than a man lay down his life for his friends. So I thank You that Jesus will be my very best friend and all my other friendships will be secondary to this one.

Father, You know the hearts of men, so I won't be deceived by outward appearances. Bad friendships corrupt good morals. So I'll be choosy about the boys and girls I'm friends with. I am asking You to give me godly friends who stick closer than a brother — quality friends who will help me build a stronger character and draw me closer to You.

I want to be a friend like David, in the Bible, a friend of those who fear You, of those who keep Your Word. Help us to talk together, laugh together, cry together, pray together, and have fun, adventure, and excitement together. Please develop a healthy, thriving social life in us, Father.

Teach me what I need to do to be a quality friend. Help me to show myself friendly to others and to love my friends at all times. Please help me to develop a fun personality and good sense of humor. Help me to relax around people and to just be myself. I don't want to be phony or uptight and scare people off. Instruct my heart and mold my character, that I may be faithful and trustworthy over the friendships You are sending into my life.

Father, thank You for helping me to meet new friends.

In Jesus' name I pray. Amen.

Scripture References

Proverbs 27:17	Ephesians 5:2,30
Proverbs 13:20	Colossians 2:2 KJV
Psalm 84:11	1 Corinthians 1:10
James 1:17	Philippians 1:27
Ecclesiastes 4:9,10	Philippians 2:2
Proverbs 18:24	John 15:13
Proverbs 17:17	Ecclesiastes 4:9
Philippians 2:3	

— 15 —

SELF-ESTEEM

Father, I come to Your throne room in order to receive help for my self-image. You created me, and that means so much to me. For I know that You always love me so I can look to You, and Your arms of love are outstretched to me. I know You didn't just carelessly or thoughtlessly throw me together, but I am wonderfully and carefully created.

Because I am Your workmanship, Your handicraft made for good works, I ask You to help me to view myself from Your perspective. Help me to realize my strengths. Open my eyes to the strengths, abilities, and talents that You have placed inside of me. Give me grace to find the good that is in me, and to be appreciative of who I am, instead of critical of who I am not.

Although the world places a huge importance on physical appearance and personality, Father, I know that You judge men's hearts. You couldn't care less about cellulite placement, or bone structure, or muscle tissue, but You're interested in a pure heart and a humble spirit. So I will not insult You by putting myself down and talking badly about myself.

Because You paid a huge price for me — the life of Your Son, Jesus — I know that I am very valuable to You. Knowing that I am chosen makes me feel special. Knowing that I am Your child and that You are my Father gives me confidence and hope. Help me to set my affections on things above rather than on things of the world. Help me to mature in my relationship with You and to develop into the happy, joyful, strong Christian that I have the potential to be. I determine not to compare myself to others.

Forgive me for thinking like the world does, Father. From now on, instead of basing my sense of self-esteem on past failures or successes, or on physical things, by the world's standards, I'll turn to Your Word. Your Word says that I am part of a royal priesthood, a holy nation. It calls me a child of God, more than a conqueror through Jesus, one who is able to do all things through Jesus Who strengthens me, because greater is He Who is in me, than he who is in the world. I am a new creation in Christ Jesus. Help me to act this way, believe this way, and talk this way, for as a man thinks in his heart, so is he.

Father, thank You for being my source of self-esteem. Although You use instruments like family members and friends to help build my sense of self-esteem, You are my main source. So I turn to You and draw my strength from You. If one source of self-esteem is dried up or goes away, I will not worry, because I still have You as my source. And I draw on You and I thank You that I can have, not an overinflated, puffed-up ego, but a healthy, strong sense of self-esteem.

My confession is that this is mine. I have it now.

In Jesus' name I pray. Amen.

Scripture References

Colossians 1:9	Psalm 139
1 Peter 4:10	Ephesians 1:4
Genesis 1:27	1 John 3:1
Hebrews 13:6	Romans 12:1
Hebrews 13:5	1 Peter 2:9
Philippians 4:13	Romans 8
Ephesians 5:2	Philippians 4:13
2 Corinthians 5:7	1 Corinthians 1:26,27
2 Corinthians 3:5	James 4:6

— 16 —

BOLDNESS

Father, help me to be bolder. Your Word says that strong boldness is a result of a strong relationship with You. The stronger my relationship with You and Jesus and the Holy Spirit, the stronger my boldness will be.

Help me not to confuse boldness with being loud, obnoxious, or rude, but to recognize that true boldness comes from knowing that I know, that I know, that I abide in Jesus and that Jesus and His Word abide in me. Boldness comes not by might nor by power, but by Your Spirit.

Father, I want to be bold with my love just as Jesus was bold with His love. Sometimes His boldness was loud, but more often than not, He had a quiet confidence and assurance that came from knowing You, and from knowing Who He was in You. Please give me the wisdom to know when to be quiet and when to speak out. Jesus loved people no one else would even talk to. Open my eyes so that I can see people as Jesus sees them. Thank You for giving me a heart of compassion and love for sinners and Christians.

I am not ashamed of You, Father, and I am not ashamed of the Gospel of Jesus Christ. Because I really love people, I am not afraid to tell them about Jesus. I need to tell people that heaven is real and so is hell. Help me to convince people that they need to ask Jesus into their hearts in order to get to heaven, because He's the only way.

Thank You for giving me the words to say, so that when I talk, it's like You, God, talking to them. I know that sometimes my actions speak so loudly that people can't hear my words, so please help me to live my faith so that my "walk" matches my "talk." Sometimes it's better not to say anything and just let people watch and see the light of love, joy, and peace in my life.

Jesus was so bold that He even gave His life. He wasn't afraid of man or beast. And so I thank You that I am not hindered by fear, because You have not given me a spirit of fear, but of power, and of love, and of a sound mind. I know that perfect love casts out all fear. So by faith, I believe that I won't be intimidated by what other people think or say. I pray for those who make fun of me. They may not receive what I have to say, but I believe that it's really Jesus they're rejecting and not just me.

Thank You for courage and strength to love and to live like Jesus. I know people made fun of Him, but He kept on going, so I'll keep on going, too.

I am asking You for boldness, wisdom, and freedom to declare Your message fearlessly at just the right time to my friends at school and at work. By faith I believe that I receive it — it's mine, I have it now. I'll continue to develop a strong relationship with You by reading Your Word, by praying, and by fellowshipping with other Christians. And I know that as I do this, I'll gain more and more boldness.

Thank You for it, Father.

In Jesus' name I pray. Amen.

Scripture References

Philippians 1:9-11

1 John 5:16,17

Romans 5:5

Mark 16:15,16

Romans 10:9,10

1 Peter 4:11

Acts 4:33

John 3:16

1 Timothy 4:2

1 John 1:9

Philippians 3:13,14

1 John 5:18

2 Corinthians 4:4

— 17 —

BEFORE A DATE*

Father, Your Word says that Jesus came that I might enjoy life to the fullest. So I thank You for the friends You have given me to date. Please teach me how to be a friend as Jesus would be. I want to bring out the very best in people, and to help them have fun and enjoy life.

Thank You for giving me different and creative ideas for things to do that are fun and exciting for us and pleasing to You. Help us not to be nervous, but to just be ourselves. So many times fear and nervousness can hinder fun and communication.

Father, I thank You that we don't have to be phony or try to be someone else. We can let our own personalities show because we are both made in Your image, with fun and interesting personalities.

I want to help my date become closer to You. I realize that I can be a positive or a negative influence on others, but I choose to be a good influence for You. I commit this relationship to You. I thank You that You've given me good judgment so that I won't form relationships with people who don't serve Jesus.

Your Word says that whatsoever is not of faith is sin, so I date by faith. I will be respectful of my date's parents, and be sure to get home on

---

*Because the Word of God instructs that children should honor and respect their parents, dating — especially among younger teens — should be with parents' permission. See Eph. 6:1-3.

time. I'll practice good manners and conduct myself like a gentleman/lady. And we will avoid the very appearance of evil. I will keep my body holy; I know that sex is good for me only if I'm married.

Your Word says that I shouldn't even associate with those who are fornicators (those who are sexually immoral). I thank You for always making a way for me to escape sin. I'll be careful not to set myself up for a fall, or to give place to the devil. I trust You for the wisdom I need in every area of my life so that I react properly to every situation.

Thank You for Your protection as we go out, because Your angels are assigned to us so we won't get hurt. I know that You hear me when I pray, so I expect to have a good date, a date filled with fun, joy, laughter, excitement, and peace. I believe that we will have an evening full of fun conversation, and I thank You that I'll have the right words to say at the end of the date.

Father, thank You for helping me to look and act my very best.

In Jesus' name I pray. Amen.

Scripture References

John 13:34,35	1 Corinthians 7:2
Ephesians 4:29	1 Corinthians 5:9-11
Psalm 139:14 KJV	2 Peter 2:9
Hebrews 10:24	Hebrews 2:18
Colossians 4:6	Psalm 91:11
Psalm 1:1	John 15:11
1 Corinthians 15:33	John 10:10
2 Corinthians 6:14-18	

— 18 —

BEFORE AN EXAM

Father, thank You for Your Word that says You've given me a spirit of love, of power, and of a sound mind. Not a defective, handicapped, weak, sickly mind, but one full of strength, vitality, and soundness. You said that I have the mind of Christ. At the age of twelve, Jesus was astonishing the religious leaders in the synagogue. It is written that Jesus grew in wisdom, strength, and favor with God and man.

I believe I have the capacity to learn and to make excellent grades. In Daniel's life, You caused him to be ten times greater in knowledge then the men of the world, when asked questions by the king. I believe that as I exercise faith in Your Word, the mind of Christ will be working in my life.

As I study, show me what to study and how to study most effectively. May the Holy Spirit cause me to be of quick understanding. Help me to develop the powers of concentration, so I can maximize the ability You have given me. Help me to discipline my mind to think on the subject matter at hand, and not daydream and lazily wander around, so I can get the most from my study time.

Father, as I enter to take this exam, I ask You to help me. Grant me wisdom and show me how to take the test, so that I gain the most points and make the best grade I can make, u   he knowledge that I have to the best   ity.

Thank You that the Holy Ghost was sent to bring things to my remembrance. So I ask and believe that those things which I might not be able to recall in my own natural ability will be brought back to my remembrance. If there is a difficult question, help me not to get frustrated or depressed, but help me to stay full of peace, for the wisdom of God is peaceable and works in a peaceful mind; I know that You will help me. I'll just answer the questions I know I can answer and come back to the harder ones later so I'll have plenty of time.

Your Word says, Father, that whatsoever is not of faith is sin, so I take my exam by faith. I will study hard and do my best. Where I come up short, I believe that You can make up the difference. I want to give glory to You in all that I do, so I'll take this test with all my heart. Because perfect love casts out all fear, I won't let fear cloud or block my thinking. I cast down those thoughts of fear and helplessness, and replace them with thoughts of faith and wisdom.

I resist any temptation to cheat on this test. I pray that everyone will work honestly and that You will help those around me to do the best they can on the exam.

In Jesus' name I pray. Amen.

Scripture References

Daniel 1:17	Ephesians 3:20
Colossians 3:23	Romans 8:37
Philippians 2:13	2 Timothy 1:7
1 Corinthians 2:16	Luke 2:40,52
Philippians 4:13	John 14:26
2 Corinthians 3:5	James 3:17
Galatians 6:9	James 1:5

— 19 —

BEFORE A SPECIAL SCHOOL EVENT

Father, I'm glad that You care about every single area of my life. You stretch out Your hand to help me whenever I ask You. So I am asking You for the wisdom and strength to be the best that I can be in this _____ event.

I don't have to worry about anything because You have not given me a spirit of fear, but of power, of love, and of a sound mind. Because Your Word says that perfect love casts out all fear, I give every worry or concern to You. And I know that You always give me grace to help me when I need it. Help me to act like Jesus in everything I do and especially in this _____ event.

By faith, I believe I can perform not only to the best of my ability, but above and beyond my natural abilities. I pray for all those who are performing with me, that we will work together and that each of us will contribute our strengths and cover each other's weaknesses.

I want people to know I'm a Christian because I act like one. I'm not looking for success in what I do just to be able to brag about it, but I realize that everything I do is a reflection of You. You give me the talents, abilities, and confidence to be successful in all that I do. Your Word says that because I am doing all things for You, and not to impress other people, I should do them with all my heart and strength.

Thank You for helping me to develop my abilities so that I can do well in all the activities I'm engaged in. Please help me to keep a good attitude during every event in which I participate. I won't let strife, hatred, or any wrong thinking enter into my mind.

Thank You, Father, for helping me to control my tongue so that everything I say and do will be a light to those people I come in contact with. Help me to handle success with poise and grace because I know that pride goes before a fall.

Lord, thank You that You made me for fellowship and friendship with You and with others; and thank You for filling my life with events that are fun and exciting.

In Jesus' name I pray. Amen.

Scripture References

James 1:5,6	1 Corinthians 15:5-7
Isaiah 41:10	2 Corinthians 2:14
Exodus 15:2	Colossians 3:23
Philippians 4:6	Joshua 1:8
1 Peter 4:11	John 13:34,35

— 20 —

BEFORE A VACATION OR A ROAD TRIP*

Father, I set my expectations and hopes upon You because You generously provide me with everything for my enjoyment. I look to You to fill me with Your joy and peace as we have fun, excitement, laughter, and adventure on this vacation/road trip. I cast all my cares upon You right now. I refuse to worry or fret about anything.

Please lead and guide me, and speak to my heart during this time away. Help me to meet and make new friends while we travel. Make me a blessing to them and use me as a witness to those I meet who don't know You. Grant me words of life to speak to their hearts so they can be born again.

As I travel, grant me eyes to see, ears to hear, and a heart to appreciate all of Your wonderful creation. Please show me those secret things that You share only with those who fear and respect You.

Thank You for granting me wisdom to handle every situation. Help me to travel intelligently and to act in a manner that is pleasing to You because I know that You are always with me and

---

*Because the Word of God instructs that children should honor and respect their parents, trips should be taken only with parents' permission — especially with younger teens. See Ephesians 6:1-3.

watching over me. Thank You for giving Your angels charge over me to keep me in all my ways. They will bear me up in their hands and encamp all around me to protect me from all harm or evil. Thank You that You protect not only my physical body, but also all of my property (auto, luggage, cameras, etc.).

Thank You, Father, that the plane, train, ship, or automobile will operate perfectly and without problems.

I'll be sure to spend time in Your Word and in prayer while I'm away, and to go to church if the opportunity arises. I thank You by faith that we'll have excellent weather, and that this will be a fun, safe, exciting, and adventurous vacation/road trip filled with laughter, rest, and relaxation — so that I can return refreshed and rejuvenated.

In Jesus' name I pray. Amen.

Scripture References

Psalm 91:10,11	Psalm 86:16
Isaiah 54:17	Philippians 4:6,7
Psalm 23:2,3 AMP	1 Timothy 6:17
Matthew 11:28	Psalm 25:14
Psalm 127:2	Romans 15:13
Acts 3:19 AMP	

— 21 —

PRAYER FOR A SPORTS EVENT

Father, I thank You that You care about all the details of my life, even this sports event. Your Word says that I am strong and can do all things because I have Jesus in my heart. I believe that You will guide my performance on the field/court/track, etc., and will not allow me to stumble.

I have practiced diligently, and You have said that the hand of the diligent shall rule. I will run this race and play this game in such a way that I might win. In Philippians 3:14 (KJV) the Apostle Paul said, **I press toward the mark for the prize of the high calling of God . . . .** In like manner I strive to win, to do my best, and to compete according to the rules in integrity and purity of heart. I'll compete with all my strength and might because I play for Your glory.

Father, I ask You for wisdom, for Your Word says that wisdom is greater than strength. Help me to compete skillfully and confidently. I believe I have the mind of Christ. Though others may look to their superior abilities, or their wealth of experience, I look to and trust in You.

I pray for my teammates. I ask that You help us play together as a team, that each one of us will contribute our individual strengths and cover one another's weaknesses. Grant our coach wisdom to make the right call at the right time. Help him/her coach effectively, inspiring us to play harder, edifying us, and building character in us.

Father, build in me the character of a godly competitor — that under pressure I may walk in peace, maintaining poise. When I am tempted to become discouraged and give up, I'll continue, empowered by Your strength. When faced with overwhelming odds, I'll not tremble in unbelief, but will walk by faith because I don't have a spirit of fear, but of power, and of love, and of a sound mind. I know that nothing is impossible with You.

And so I believe I can play not only to the best of my ability, but also above and beyond my ability, because I play and compete by faith. And because faith works by love, I will not murmur, complain, gossip, or get offended at the officials, coaches, opposing team, or at my own team if something happens that I don't like.

When graced with victory, I'll not become prideful, because pride goes before a fall, but will gratefully give You all the glory. And if by some chance we should lose, I will resist the temptation to become discouraged, because I know that You always cause us to triumph in Christ Jesus, and that we are winners through Jesus.

Father, thank You that both teams can play free from injury. I pray that this will be a fair game and a just game. Thank You that the officials will be fair and impartial and will keep all things decent and in order.

Thank You that I can do all things through Christ Who strengthens me. No matter what the results of this game, I will exercise the fruit of the Spirit and be a gracious athlete.

In Jesus' name I pray. Amen.

Scripture References

Proverbs 4:12	Philippians 4:13
1 Corinthians 2:16	Ecclesiastes 9:10
Isaiah 40:31	Ecclesiastes 9:16
Psalm 91:12	Colossians 3:23
Galatians 5:22	

— 22 —

PART-TIME OR FULL-TIME JOB*

Father, thank You that You are my Provider and Source of total supply. Every good thing that I have comes from You. I believe You will show me a way to earn money so that I can help spread the Gospel to every nation.

I ask in the name of Jesus for a job that pays enough to meet all of my financial needs. Your Word says that it is good for me to enjoy the results of my work. It is a gift from You that I am happy where I work. It is my goal to do my best on my job so that I will gain the respect and favor of my co-workers and my employers. Help me not to grow tired of doing what is right. Teach me the best way to manage my money so that I won't waste or throw it away.

I thank You, Father, that You are leading me to the best possible job. Thank You for a job that will work well and not conflict with my relationship with You, or with any of my family, school, or church priorities.

Help me to develop a strong work ethic and to have an excellent and enthusiastic attitude. Help me to be obedient to my employer. If something goes against my conscience, help me to be bold and clear in my communication to the

---

*Because the Word of God instructs that children should honor their parents, having a part-time or full-time job should be with parents' permission — especially with younger teens. See Ephesians 6:1-3.

people who can change things so that it won't make a bad scene. Help me to be an effective witness for the Gospel. I'll work hard, diligently, and quietly with an humble spirit at all times, not just when my boss is around, but as if I were working for You, because I am working for You.

Thank You that I am strong because of You, Father. I will not give up, but I trust that my work will be recognized and rewarded. By faith, I work twice as hard as everyone else so that some day when promotions come, I can make twice as much money.

Thank You for Your protection so I don't have to be nervous or afraid of anything, but I share my requests with You in prayer. Thanks for Your peace that protects my heart and mind in every situation.

Father, please help me to have absolute and complete control over my tongue, what I say, so that I won't hurt or offend anyone. I won't murmur, complain, backbite, or gossip, because I know that these are some of the things that kept the children of Israel out of the promised land.

Thank You that I have favor with my boss and all of the people I work with.

In Jesus' name I pray. Amen.

Scripture References

Deuteronomy 8:18 1 Thessalonians 4:11,12
Isaiah 48:17 KJV 2 Thessalonians 3:12,13
James 1:5 2 Chronicles 15:7
Philippians 4:19 Philippians 4:6,7
Ephesians 6:5-7 Ecclesiastes 5:18,19 KJV,NIV

— 23 —

YOUR FUTURE

Father, I'm dedicated to You and to live for You.

I don't know everything the future holds for me, but I know that You hold my future; You can see the end from the beginning. I trust You to lead me, to be my guide in life through the Holy Spirit Who lives inside me. If I don't feel right about something in my heart, then I won't do it until You give me peace in my heart. Help me to do the things in life that You have for me to do. I trust You to prepare me now for the things that are to come, and to give me wisdom to discern the right timing for what You would have me do in each season of my life.

As I follow You by faith, Father, I know that my future is bright and exciting. The possibilities and my potential are limitless if I stay close to You in Your Word and prayer. I can have an extraordinary life filled with excitement, adventure, and fun if I follow Your leading. On the other hand, I can have a future filled with boredom, regret, and pain if I reject You. The choice is mine. I choose to love, obey, and cleave unto You with my whole body, soul, and spirit.

If college is in my future, please help me to select the right one. Provide the way for me to go. If it's not college, then prepare me for my job. Help me to recognize the skills You have given me so that I can develop them and give the glory to You. Give me understanding and light so that

I am quick to learn. I thank You for the wisdom and light that come from You and Your Word.

I'm not afraid of anything You have in store for me. You are a help to me in everything I do. When the time for marriage comes, if that is Your will for me, I thank You that You are not only preparing me, but You are also working on my future spouse. But until that time comes, help me to be content in every situation.

Lord, You know that it takes money to do just about anything. So I believe that You will supply all the money I need to do Your will. Where You guide, You provide. So I commit to do Your Word and work hard in school, and I believe that You will see that all of my needs are met. I believe You will instruct me and teach me which way to go. You don't make things confusing for me, but You make a clear path for me when I put You first. Confusion and fear come from the devil, so I won't be motivated by them.

Thank You for Your words which are a light for my path and for Your Holy Spirit Who navigates me along Your way. I may not know exactly what the future has for me, but one thing I do know for sure — that I'll always love You, and follow You, and seek You, and spend time with You in Your Word and prayer, and share Your love with others.

So I won't speak words of confusion, doubt, or unbelief when asked, "What are you going to do?" My confession is, "I'll do the right thing!" I know that important things are seldom urgent and little urgent things are seldom important. So I won't be hasty, but I'll be calm and stay in Your Word and prayer about my future so that when the time comes for me to take a step of faith, I can do it confidently.

Thank You, Father, for holding me and my future in the palm of Your hand.

In Jesus' name I pray. Amen.

Scripture References

Jeremiah 33:3	Hebrews 13:5
John 16:13	Romans 8:14
1 Timothy 4:14	Psalm 32:8
Psalm 25:5	Proverbs 3:5,6
Ephesians 1:16-18; 2:10	Psalm 119:105
1 Peter 5:7	1 Corinthians 2:9,10
Philippians 4:19	Deuteronomy 30:20
Luke 10:7	John 10:10

— 24 —

DEDICATION FOR YOUR TITHES

I profess this day unto You, Father, that I have come into the inheritance which You swore to give me. I am in the land which You have provided for me in Jesus Christ, the Kingdom of Almighty God. I was a sinner serving Satan; he was my god. But I called upon the name of Jesus, and You heard my cry and delivered me into the Kingdom of Your dear Son.

Jesus, as my Lord and High Priest, I bring the first 10 percent of my income to You and worship the Lord my God with it.

I rejoice in all the good which You have given to me and my family. I have listened to the voice of the Lord my God and have done according to all that He has commanded me.

Thank You for opening the windows of heaven and pouring out a blessing on me that I can hardly contain. I believe that You have rebuked Satan from devouring what You have given me.

I thank You, Father.

In Jesus' name I pray. Amen.

Scripture References

Deuteronomy 26:1,3,10,11,14,15

Malachi 3:10

Ephesians 2:1-5

Colossians 1:13

Hebrews 3:1,7,8

75

— 25 —

PEACEFUL SLEEP

In the name of Jesus, I bind you, Satan, and all your agents from my dreams. I forbid you to interfere in any way with my sleep.

If I can't sleep, I don't count sheep — I talk to the Shepherd. So I bring every thought, every imagination, and every dream into the captivity and obedience of Jesus Christ.

Father, I thank You that even as I sleep my heart counsels me and reveals to me Your purpose and plan. Thank You for a peaceful sleep, for You promised Your beloved sweet sleep. Therefore, my heart is glad, and my spirit rejoices. My body and soul rest and confidently sleep in safety.

Thank You for Your angels surrounding my bed and protecting me from any evil or danger.

In Jesus' name I pray. Amen.

Scripture References

Matthew 16:19   Psalm 16:7-9
Matthew 18:18   Psalm 127:2
2 Corinthians 10:5   Proverbs 3:24
Psalm 91   Psalm 23

Part III

PRAYERS FOR OTHERS

— 26 —

PARENTS AND FAMILY

Father, I bring my parents and family before You in prayer. Thank You that we have been blessed with all spiritual blessings in Christ Jesus. Your Word says that it takes wisdom to build a family and understanding to make it strong. I ask that You make my parents strong and wise. Please fill them with the knowledge that they need in order to build a strong, healthy relationship together.

Help Dad to act and speak in love toward Mom even when he doesn't feel like it. Help Mom to submit to the loving leadership of Dad. Help them to communicate with one another and pray with each other that their relationship may thrive, so they can be more in love now than they were when they were first married.

I pray that my brothers, sisters, and I will obey, honor, and respect our parents' authority, that we may live in peace and quiet so that things will go well with us and we will live a long life on this earth. I pray that my family is founded and securely built upon Your Word, like the house that was founded upon the rock and built so securely that when the flood came the house couldn't be shaken.

Help Dad to be the spiritual leader of our house and grant him the wisdom he needs to raise us with faith, encouragement, and love. Please give Dad and Mom the insight to know when and how to discipline us so that we turn out right. Help Dad to guide our household so that he may boldly proclaim, "As for me and my house, we will serve the Lord."

Help us to bear with each other and forgive each other, as You have forgiven us, and to love each other as You have loved us. Love wraps us all together in perfect unity. I want the peace of God to rule in our hearts. Open our eyes that we may realize the gift of God that is in each one of us, so that we no longer view one another from a human point of view, but from Your point of view. Help us to value, respect, and be grateful for each other, instead of taking each other for granted. Because we are members of one body, we are called to work together peacefully.

Father, I pray that my parents and family and I will always choose to serve You, and that our hearts are knit together in love. I pray that our home will be a place of safety and refuge, a place of encouragement filled with laughter, happiness, love, and joy.

Thank You so much for providing for all of our physical, emotional, and financial needs. Thank You for giving Your angels charge over us so that our home is safe from all danger, harm, or evil.

In Jesus' name I pray. Amen.

Scripture References

Proverbs 24:3 EB	John 15:12
Philippians 2:2	Colossians 2:2
Ephesians 5:21,22,25	Colossians 3:15
1 Timothy 2:2	Joshua 24:15
Luke 6:48	Deuteronomy 12:12
Ephesians 6:1-3	2 Corinthians 5:16
Colossians 3:13,14	Proverbs 15:17
Psalm 112:1,3 AMP,NIV,EB	

BOYFRIEND/GIRLFRIEND*

Father, I know that You care about every area of my life, even who I date. So I believe that _____ is blessed with all spiritual blessings in Christ Jesus. Thank You that he/she is a friend I can grow with, learn from, and have fun with.

I know that as we put You first and keep our relationship with You close through Your Word and prayer, You will bless this relationship. Help us to communicate with each other so we will have an understanding of the differences between the way men and women think and see things.

Thank You for bringing _____ into my life so we can encourage each other to grow closer to You, Father. Help me to be a blessing to him/her so that I can contribute something valuable into his/her life. Thank You that he/she will like me for who I am, and love You because of Who You are. I pray that _____ will stay on fire for You and love Jesus more and more, so that we can grow closer to You and minister to other people.

I know that bad friends corrupt and destroy good morals. Help _____ to say no to bad friends and to have You as his/her first love. You comfort him/her when no one else can.

---

*Because the Word of God instructs that children should honor and respect their parents, dating — especially with younger teens — should be with parents' permission. See Eph. 6:1-3.

Help him/her to be content in his/her relationship with You. You are his/her friend when everyone else leaves. I thank You for the Holy Spirit Who will warn him/her of bad situations and lead him/her into good situations.

Help us not to compromise our relationship with You for a cheap thrill. If Your Spirit says no, we'll obey immediately, because sin thrills but then it kills; it fascinates and then it assassinates.

Father, help _____ to be a doer of the Word. Help us to treat each other with purity in our relationship. Help us to keep our relationship in perspective; we are brother and sister in the Lord and help us to act accordingly. If I wouldn't do an activity with my natural brother/sister, help me not to do it with _____.

My spouse will be my lover; my date is my sister/brother in You, Lord. I pray that our relationship will be a healthy one, bringing growth and maturity to both of our lives. And thank You that _____ has favor and a good relationship with my family, because I know that this is important to You.

Most people get so uptight about relationships. Help us just to relax and be friends.

Father, I pray that we will always listen to Your voice and that we will always be sensitive to Your Spirit so that we don't set ourselves up for a fall. So if we don't need to be in this relationship, I thank You that You will reveal this to us quickly, so that we can do the right thing and just keep being friends.

Thank You for Your angels who are protecting
_____ from all harm, evil, or danger.
Thank You for what You are doing in
_____'s life.

In Jesus' name I pray. Amen.

Scripture References

1 Peter 5:7   John 14:18
James 1:5   Romans 8:14
Psalm 37:4   Romans 6:23
1 Corinthians 15:33

YOUR FUTURE SPOUSE

(If someday you want to be married)

Lord, Your Word says that it is not good that I should be alone, so I believe it is Your will that I be married someday.

Father, Your Word also says that You desire that I live a life free from care, that I should be content and satisfied in every situation that I am in, and that I should not be anxious or worried about anything. If I am willing and obedient to Your Word, You will give me the desires of my heart.

It is my desire that someday I will be married to a person I am attracted to and love, and who loves me. Because my future spouse is somewhere in the earth right now, by faith, I pray for him/her.

Father, especially help him/her to grow in love, Your kind of love. A friend loves at all times, and I desire for my spouse to be my very best friend. I desire that my spouse be a person who shares the same love that I have for You, someone who will be one in spirit and purpose with me.

I ask You to send mature men and women into our lives to give us good, godly counsel and to teach us how we should love each other and care for our family. Teach us both what You expect husbands and wives to do and how we ought to behave toward each other. Reveal to our hearts Your Word concerning the marriage relationship and correct any wrong thinking in our lives. Grant us knowledge through godly people, books, tapes, and preaching that will give us understanding concerning relationships, so that we can avoid many of the common errors and mistakes people tend to make.

Father, You are omnipresent (everywhere at all times) so You know where my future spouse is right now. It may even be someone I already know. I trust You to lead me and guide me by Your Holy Spirit so that when Your perfect time is right, I will have the wisdom, discretion, and discernment to know when I have found someone who is compatible with me. Not only will he/she be good for me, I thank You that I will be good for him/her.

Help me not to be over (or under) spiritual in my choice, but to rely on the mind and the spirit that You've given me.

I pray that the eyes of my future spouse's understanding will be opened so that he/she will have complete knowledge of Your will in all spiritual wisdom and understanding. I pray that he/she will live a life that is worthy of You, Lord, and pleasing to You in every way. Thank You that he/she will always be involved in doing good deeds, and have a stronger, growing relationship with You.

Thank You for commanding Your angels to surround my future spouse, protecting him/her from any harm, danger, or evil.

Father, as I wait on Your timing, I will prepare myself for marriage. And as I date (as my parents permit) and develop stronger social and relationship skills, I determine to keep myself holy and pure from sexual sin. I will save myself for my future mate. I determine that I won't scare people off by being uptight, worried, or desperate for marriage, but I'll act in faith and patience and be happy, content, and satisfied until that time.

My hope and my happiness are in You, Father. Thank You for my future mate.

In Jesus' name I pray. Amen.

Scripture References

Philippians 2:2-7

Ephesians 5:22-25

Galatians 5:22,23

Colossians 1:9,10

Psalm 37:4,5

Psalm 130:5

Genesis 2:18-24

Titus 2:3-5

FRIENDS AND CLASSMATES

Father, I thank You for all of my friends and classmates. I believe that You are able to do exceeding abundantly above all that I ask or think, so I am believing for some outstanding relationships in my life.

I pray for the friends You have already blessed me with. Help us to be faithful in our relationships with each other, and to be trustworthy with the secrets we share. Help us to be loving toward each other at all times, even when we may disappoint each other. Help us to challenge each other in our walk with You so that we develop in character and sharpen each other as iron sharpens iron. Grant us times of heart-to-heart talks and times when we can correct each other if we need to. Help us to love each other as You have loved us, and to be sensitive to one another, laying down our own lives and being unselfish by taking the time to pray for each other. May our hearts be strengthened as they are knit together in Your love.

Father, please help my friends to live their lives as You want them to so that they will always please You. Open the eyes of their understanding so that the spirit of wisdom and revelation will be upon them, so that they can see that You're able to do exceeding abundantly above all that they ask or think. I ask You to bless them and touch everything they do so that it is successful and prosperous. Thank You for helping them to have great family relationships. Help them to have favor with You, with their teachers, and with all other people.

I thank You that the devil can't keep them from seeing the light of Jesus and the salvation that Jesus brings. Thank You for giving them undeserved favor and spiritual strength and a better understanding of Jesus. I believe that Your angels will watch over and protect them from any harm or evil in the world. Thank You for providing for their every financial need and helping them to always triumph in Jesus.

In Jesus' name I pray. Amen.

Scripture References

2 Corinthians 4:4	Galatians 5:22
2 Peter 3:18 AMP	Ephesians 6:19
Proverbs 3:7	John 12:32
Philippians 1:9-11	1 John 3:24
Isaiah 54:17	Exodus 23:25,26
Psalm 91:10,11,16	John 3:16
Matthew 9:38	Colossians 2:2
Ephesians 6:10,11	Proverbs 27:5,6,9

— 30 —

UNBELIEVERS AT SCHOOL

Father, when Jesus gave us the Great Commission, He said, "Go into all the world and preach the Gospel to every creature." The Apostle Paul said, "How can people call on someone they don't believe in? And how can they believe in someone if they haven't heard of him? And how can they hear unless someone preaches to them?"

I am asking You, Father, to send forth laborers, including me, into my school. Cause us to be bold and filled with the Spirit, that we may be fearless in speech, and behave in such a way that we do all things pleasing in Your sight. Help my life to be a positive testimony for You to use. Give me opportunities to tell others of all that Jesus has done. I am asking You for the outpouring of the Holy Spirit at my school, that the manifestations of the Holy Spirit will be in operation, to turn people's attention toward You.

I thank You for revival in the hearts of every Christian at my school, Lord. I pray that there will be a love for You, a love for prayer, and for Your Word — a new love for the things of God and a new love for souls — so that Christians won't just sit around, but will begin to share Your love with those who are lost.

Father, Your Word says that supernatural signs will follow those who believe in Jesus' name. So I believe that these signs will follow us wherever we go.

I ask that the blinders will be removed from the eyes of the people at my school. I pray specifically for _____. And I ask You to give me an anointing that I will know how to speak a timely word to him/her. I ask that his/her eyes and heart will be opened to know that there is a heaven to gain and a hell to avoid. Send me with Your Word to open his/her eyes and to help turn him/her from darkness to light and from the power of Satan to the power of God, so that he/she may receive forgiveness of sins, and make Jesus his/her Lord.

Father, I ask You to give me the sinners at my school as my inheritance. Use me to get them born again and filled with the Spirit. I have been given authority over the devil, so I bind Satan in Jesus' name from interfering with the Word of God reaching these people. I break his power over them and command him to loose his assignment over them.

I know that if I ask anything according to Your will, You hear me; and if I know that You hear me, I know that I have what I have asked of You. Thank You for working in the lives of the people for whom I am praying. Thank You for revival at my school.

In Jesus' name I pray. Amen.

Every day after praying this prayer, thank the Lord for the salvation of your schoolmates. Rejoice and praise God for the victory! Confess the above prayer as done! Thank God for sending the laborers. Thank Him that Satan is bound. Alleluia!

Scripture References

Matthew 9:37	1 John 5:14,15
2 Corinthians 3:6	Isaiah 50:4
2 Corinthians 4:3,4	Isaiah 51:16
Ephesians 1:18	Psalm 2:8
Acts 26:17,18	Mark 16:15-18
Luke 10:19	Romans 10:14
Matthew 18:18	Isaiah 50:4
2 Timothy 2:26	Isaiah 51:16
Job 22:30	

— 31 —

TEACHERS AT SCHOOL

Father, I thank You for my teachers. Please cause them to be a positive influence on the lives of the students. Help them to make learning fun, and to capture the attention of their classes in creative ways. I pray that they will able to control the rebellious, calm the violent, motivate the lazy, direct the zealous, encourage the weak, and love the unloved.

I pray that if _____ is not born again, and does not have a personal relationship with Your Son Jesus, You will send someone to share Jesus with him/her and open his/her eyes to turn him/her from darkness to the light.

I pray that my teachers will skillfully develop the ability and knowledge You have given them. Please teach them and guide them in how and what they should teach so they can prepare us for what we will face when we graduate. I pray that they will have the respect of their students.

Father, I ask that You give my teachers insight and understanding into the lives of the students in the class, so that they can help them with any problems they may be facing.

I ask that You lead and guide my teachers into Your truth. I pray that You help them to have a strong relationship with You.

Thank You for encouraging them when they are upset and discouraged in their jobs. Help them to see the importance of their work in educating us. Give my teachers strength so they will not be tired of doing what is right. Help them enjoy and experience the results of their persistence. Please bless them and their families, and prosper them financially so that they will have all their needs met. Protect them from any evil, danger, or injury.

Father, I pray You will always guide my teachers to follow Your plan and uphold godliness in the classroom. Thank You that they have favor with their students and with their bosses.

In Jesus' name I pray. Amen.

Scripture References

Psalm 119:130

Exodus 31:3,4

2 Corinthians 3:5

Proverbs 4:5

Psalm 32:8

Acts 26:17,18

Matthew 9:38

Proverbs 4:8

Ephesians 6:10,11

Galatians 6:9

Philippians 2:13 KJV

— 32 —

PASTOR AND YOUTH PASTOR

Father, You said that You would give us shepherds according to Your heart, pastors who will feed us with knowledge and understanding. So I thank You for my pastor and youth pastor. I receive and respect them as a gift from You. I ask You to give them a heart for the people in the congregation. Inspire and anoint them so they will feed us truth from Your Word.

You said that the Good Shepherd gives his life for the sheep. Help them lay down their lives for us as we submit our lives to them. Teach them how to instruct and perfect us so that we can do the work of the ministry.

I ask You, Father, that they may have a heart of compassion for those who are lost, that we may all effectively reach out to our community. Give them creativity to declare the Gospel and minister to the congregation in a way that is anointed and interesting.

Help their love to grow in knowing and understanding You so they can be completely sure of what is Your best.

Grant my pastor and youth pastor a fresh anointing of Your wisdom, understanding, counsel, power, and knowledge. Give them times of fun, rest, and relaxation so they can be refreshed and rejuvenated.

Father, I ask that they may clearly share with others Your Son's salvation and bring Your healing to all those with broken hearts, and all who need healing. By the power of Your Spirit, help them to set people free from all the oppression of the devil.

As they spend time with You, speak and reveal to them from Your Word truth that will set us free. Show them clearly and exactly what You would have them to do — how they are to guide the congregation. Show them Your plan and Your purpose and the goals that they should pursue.

I ask that You give them freedom to speak, that they may boldly declare what You have placed in their hearts, that they may speak as the oracles of God, and be strengthened with Your anointing.

I pray that they will always walk in and teach Your love. Please help them understand and guard the responsibility You have given them over our church and youth group. Help my pastor and youth pastor understand Your will and live a life worthy of the Gospel with purity and holiness. May they and their families be protected by Your great power so that they will not be hurt.

Thank You for blessing my pastor, youth pastor, and our church financially so we can do what You have called us to do.

In Jesus' name I pray. Amen.

Scripture References

Ephesians 3:17-19
Philippians 1:9
Ephesians 3:18
Isaiah 11:2,3
Luke 4:18 NIV, KJV, AMP
Ephesians 4:15
Ephesians 6:19
2 Corinthians 3:6 NIV, KJV
2 Timothy 1:13,14

1 Peter 5:2,3
Jeremiah 3:15
Jeremiah 23:4
John 10:11
Matthew 9:36
John 8:31,32
Psalm 23:2,3
Colossians 1:9-11
Isaiah 54:17

— 33 —

LEADERS OF OUR COUNTRY

Father, thank You for the United States and its government. I pray for the president, the national and local government, the judges, the policemen, the business leaders, and all those who are in leadership positions in this country. Please protect them from the evil that is in the world and keep them safe and free from all harm.

Your Word says that when good men are in authority, the people celebrate, but when wicked men are in authority, the people are unhappy. I pray that You will keep good men and women in authority over my country. I ask that You promote and raise up a generation of able politicians who are men and women of truth, full of wisdom, and respectful towards You.

You have promised to bless any nation that follows after You. Help us to live quiet and peaceful lives so that we can continue to spread the Good News of the Gospel throughout the United States and the world.

I also pray that You give the men and women in leadership positions the understanding, wisdom, and ability to keep this country in order. I ask that You guide the president's heart and cause him to make decisions that will promote godliness. Please keep evil and wicked men from influencing the president. Keep his office based on things that are right.

Father, I pray for my brothers and sisters in the Lord who are in positions of leadership. I ask You to strengthen them in their hearts with all might by Your Spirit. Cause them to be bold and courageous. Surround them with favor as a shield, and expand their godly influence.

I pray for those in leadership positions who are not born again and who do not have a personal relationship with Your Son, Jesus. I pray that You will send someone to share Jesus with them and open their eyes to the light.

I pray for the Supreme Court. I ask that the men and women make righteous judgments, that they reach just and fair conclusions. Help the judges to inquire diligently, that they may make sound decisions. Turn their hearts to change past decisions and make new decisions that uphold goodness and godliness in our nation. If there is anyone who refuses godliness, I ask that he/she may be removed and replaced by one who respects godliness.

I ask that You cause the leaders of this country to make decisions that increase the integrity of our nation. Grant them the wisdom and insight needed to deal with this nation's finances, that You may cause us to prosper and be a blessing to other nations.

May Your Word multiply in our nation's capital so that our leaders may be better able to cooperate with Your plan and purpose.

Father, use this nation and its leaders in this great harvest of souls that will take place in the last days. I praise and thank You for blessing my country. I pray that our nation will accomplish the things that You want us to accomplish. I thank You that Jesus is Lord over the United States of America.

In Jesus' name I pray. Amen.

Scripture References

1 Timothy 2:1-3

Proverbs 29:2 KJV

Psalm 33:12

Proverbs 21:1

Proverbs 20:28

Matthew 13:39

Proverbs 25:5

Proverbs 4:10-14

Proverbs 2:10-14,20,21

— 34 —

COMFORT FOR A PERSON WHO HAS LOST A LOVED ONE

Father, in the name of Jesus I come boldly to Your throne of grace to obtain mercy and comfort for _____ in this time of need. I ask that the Holy Spirit comfort, soothe, and heal his/her broken heart.

Please give me the right words to say because I don't want to say anything that is trite or that will bring confusion. I only want to say words that will minister life and peace to his/her heart. Help me to be quiet and say nothing if that is the best thing for me to do.

Father, I want to comfort those who need it, as You have comforted me. Help me to weep with those who weep. Your Word says that those who mourn are blessed by You, and will be comforted. Jesus was sent to heal the brokenhearted, so thank You for comforting and healing _____'s heart and letting him/her feel Your presence in a new and stronger way. Help him/her to be able to get on with his/her life after a normal grieving process.

In the name of Jesus, I bind any spirit of depression, guilt, or suicide that would try to attach itself to _____ and cause him/her to be paralyzed by grief and despair.

Thank You for lifting _____ up and giving him/her laughter for tears, and happiness and joy for sadness and mourning. Help him/her to look to You for comfort and to offer You praise for Your promise of renewed life.

If the loved one was a Christian, please help _____ to see that the departed is in heaven and in a much, much better place with You. And if _____ is not sure about where the loved one has gone, help him/her, Father, to make sure of his/her own salvation.

I pray now that if _____ is not born again, and does not have a personal relationship with Jesus, You will send someone to share Jesus with him/her and open his/her eyes to the light.

Finally, I ask that You help _____ find Your peace and joy in this situation. I thank You that You are reassuring him/her that You are his/her strength. Show _____ that although people will leave, Jesus is a friend Who sticks closer than a brother, and that You will never leave nor forsake him/her.

I thank You, Father, for these things.

In Jesus' name I pray. Amen.

Scripture References

Hebrews 4:15,16 AMP   Isaiah 61:3
2 Corinthians 1:3,4   Psalm 119:50
Romans 12:15   2 Corinthians 4:4
Matthew 5:4   Nehemiah 8:10
Luke 4:18

— 35 —

DELIVERANCE OF A PERSON FROM A CULT

Father, in the name of Jesus, I come before You in prayer and in faith believing that Your Word runs swiftly throughout the earth. I bring _____ (all those and their families who are involved in cults) before You in prayer.

Stretch forth Your hand from above; rescue and deliver _____ out of danger, from this cult. The mouths of these people must be stopped for they are mentally deceiving _____ by teaching evil for the purpose of satisfying the flesh. But, praise God, they will not get very far, for their evil stupidity will become obvious to everybody!

Execute justice, Father, for _____. Set the prisoners free, open the eyes of the blind, lift up the hurting, heal the brokenhearted, and bind up their wounds. Lift up the humble and needy and cast the wicked down to the ground in the mighty name of Jesus.

Turn back the hearts of the disobedient and unpersuadable to the wisdom of the upright, and the knowledge of Your will.

Father, You say in Your Word to refrain our voices from weeping and our eyes from tears, for our prayers will be rewarded and _____ will return from this cult and come again to his/her own family. We will see _____ walking in the ways of Jesus, respecting Your name. Those who err in spirit will come to understanding. Those who murmur and complain will accept instruction in Jesus. Lord, You contend with those who contend with us, and You give safety to _____.

Satan, I speak to you in the name of Jesus. I bind you, the principalities, the powers, the rulers of the darkness, and wicked spirits in heavenly places, and I tear down strongholds using the mighty weapons God has provided for us in the name of Jesus. I speak to any demon spirit involved and break your assignment against _____. I cancel all negative talking and doubt and unbelief. Satan, you will not use this against _____.

I commission the angels to go forth and dispel these forces of darkness and bring _____ home in the name of Jesus. I believe and say that _____ has had knowledge of and been acquainted with the Word which is able to instruct him/her and give him/her the understanding for salvation which comes through faith in Christ Jesus. I pray and believe that You certainly will deliver _____ and draw _____ to Yourself from every assault of evil, and that You will preserve and bring _____ safe into Your heavenly Kingdom.

Glory to You, Father, Who delivers those for whom we intercede.

In Jesus' name I pray. Amen.

Once this prayer has been prayed for an individual, confess it as done. Thank the Father that he/she is delivered, returning from the enemy's land. Thank

God that Satan is bound. Thank God for his/her salvation.

Scripture References

Psalm 147:15	Isaiah 43:5,6
2 Timothy 2:9	Isaiah 29:23,24
Psalm 144:7,8	Isaiah 49:25
Titus 1:11	Matthew 18:18
2 Timothy 3:9	2 Timothy 3:2-9
Psalm 146:7,8	Hebrews 1:14
Psalm 147:3-6	2 Timothy 3:15
Luke 1:17	2 Timothy 4:18
Jeremiah 31:16,17	Job 22:30
Jeremiah 46:27	

Part IV

SPECIAL PRAYERS

— 36 —

VICTORY OVER FEAR*

Father, I come to Your throne boldly, in the mighty name of Jesus. I ask You to help me to overcome fear. I give You all of the worries and problems I am facing right now.

Lord, I trust You to work out all things for my good, because I love You and am following You. Thank You so much for Jesus, Who defeated the devil, the maker of fear. Because of Jesus, I can have a good life, and the devil can't steal, kill, or destroy anything that You have given me. I believe that no weapon that is aimed at me can hurt me.

I will not be captive to the devil's fear any longer. Jesus came to set the captives free, and if the Son has made me free, I am free indeed. I know the truth and it's the truth of Your Word that makes me free. You are my strength and my refuge, so I can boldly say, "The Lord is my Helper. I will not fear or be terrified, for what can man do to me?"

When the devil comes against me to try to make me afraid, I will resist him and he must flee from me, because he is a liar and the father of lies. And I will not listen to his deception or be in bondage to his fear any more, because Jesus has already defeated the devil and embarrassed him openly.

Therefore I take my place in Christ and I believe in my heart that You have not given me

---

*See the prayer for "Controlling Your Thoughts/Renewing Your Mind."

a spirit of fear — not a weakly, feeble, cowardly spirit — but a spirit of power and strength — an overcomer's spirit. You've given me a spirit of love, the kind of love that never fails; because perfect love casts out all fear and is always victorious.

Lord, You've given me a sound mind — a mind not dominated by fearful, self-defeating thoughts — but a mind fixed on the truth that the Greater One is inside of me. I am more than a conqueror through Christ. Thanks be to God Who always leads me to victory. I can do all things through Christ Who strengthens me. When Satan attacks me with fear, I'll fight back with the sharp sword of Your Word. Your Word is alive and full of power; it pulls down the strongholds of fear in my life.

So I speak to that spirit of fear. In the name of Jesus it must leave me alone. I will not be terrified by my enemies, for I am convinced that if God is for me, no one can successfully stand against me. This hour I stand as a righteous man/woman, bold as a lion. For You are with me, Lord. I refuse to look at circumstances in terror, for You are my God. I believe You will strengthen me and toughen me up so that I can go through difficulties without fear. Yes, You will hold me up with Your right hand. As I resist the devil's tactics of fear steadfastly in faith, the devil must flee from me.

Father, thank You so much for freedom from fear.

In Jesus' name I pray. Amen.

Scripture References

Isaiah 51:12,13   Psalm 91:1,10,11

Psalm 34:4   Proverbs 3:25,26

1 Peter 5:7   Isaiah 41:10

Philippians 4:6   Philippians 4:7

Romans 8:28   Philippians 1:27

Colossians 2:15   Proverbs 28:1

John 10:10   James 4:7

2 Timothy 1:7

VICTORY OVER PRIDE

Father, Your Son Jesus said that I should let my light so shine before men that they will see my good deeds and glorify You. Please help me to resist the temptation to bask in the attention that comes with a victorious life. Help me to turn the praise and admiration of my friends and peers toward the One Who truly deserves it — You.

Help me to see things the way they really are so that I can be balanced. Everything I have and everything I'm able to do is because of You. In myself I can do nothing; I have nothing; and I know nothing — without You, I am nothing. But I am glad that I am not without You, and that with You and through You I can do all things. Nothing is impossible to me because I believe Your Word. All I have, I've received from You. All that I know, You have taught me. All that I am, I am by Your grace.

Father, please teach me how I can be humble without losing my personality and the uniqueness You placed within me. Help me not to yield to the deceitfulness of pride, especially in the midst of success when everything is going great. Help me to realize the good in me and realize that You are the One Who is responsible for giving it to me. Your Word says that a man's pride shall bring him low or tear him down, but that honor will lift up the humble in spirit.

Even Satan could have had right standing before You if he had not fallen into the evil sin of pride. Help me to keep things in perspective so that I'll not fall into that sin. With Your help, I'll be balanced. I won't think too highly or too lowly of myself. I don't want to be puffed up, or have the big head, but I don't want to have a false humility either — one that says, "You're no good" or "You're unworthy." I'll see myself as You and Your Word see me — sanctified, justified, purified, glorified, beautified, and satisfied.

I respect You, Lord, and I hate sin, pride, arrogance, and every evil way. Pride goes before destruction, embarrassment, and disgrace, but wisdom comes from humility. Pride is a strange sickness because it makes the person who has it feel good, and it makes everybody else feel sick.

Help me to behave gracefully around others with humility of mind, so that when people compliment me, I can graciously say "thank you" without building myself up or putting myself down. I'll be sure to give You all the glory.

Let my successes be a testimony of the grace of God.

In Jesus' name I pray. Amen.

Scripture References

1 Corinthians 4:4 KJV	1 Peter 5:5,6
2 Corinthians 3:5	1 Timothy 3:6
Philippians 4:13	Romans 12:3
James 4:6	Proverbs 8:13
1 Corinthians 15:10	Proverbs 11:2
James 4:10	Isaiah 29:19
Proverbs 29:23	Psalm 37:11

111

— 38 —

OVERCOMING INTIMIDATION

Father, Your Word says that I have the victory in every situation. It declares that I am more than a conqueror through Jesus, so I will not be intimidated by anyone. Nobody is greater than You, Father. Greater are You Who lives in me than he who is in the world.

You are my rock and my fortress. Your name is a strong tower that I can run into and be safe. When I need to be saved from my enemies, I call on You and You save me. You will deliver me into peace from this situation I am now facing. I am not afraid and I will not be ashamed. You will not allow me to be humiliated because You always cause me to triumph in Christ Jesus.

Your Word says that You have not given me a spirit of fear, but of power, and of love, and of a sound mind. You have said that You will cause my enemies who rise up against me to be defeated before my face; they will come out against me one way and will flee before me seven ways. My weapons are not like worldly weapons, but they are stronger and more powerful through God to pull down this stronghold of intimidation.

I am not afraid of man nor beast because You have given me dominion even over the beasts of the field.

Father, even though those who are against me may be stronger than I am, I refuse to be afraid and intimidated by them. It doesn't matter how strong the intimidation may be, I will stay confident. I am not afraid because You are always with me, and You will never leave me nor forsake me. I will not become upset, because You are my God. And if You are for me, who can stand against me? When I need strength, You always give it to me.

Although I always treat with honor, respect, and dignity those who are older and in authority over me, I don't need to be intimidated by them.

Thank You that they who are opposing me will be ashamed and that their opposition will disappear. I have no reason to worry about those who do not like me. I also will not envy those people who do evil things. I'll always delight in You, and You will give me the desires of my heart.

I am committed to You, Father. I trust in You, Lord. I am determined to walk in love and not to strike back in fear or anger. But I forgive and pray for my persecutors and ask that You take the blinders off their eyes so they can see how much You love them. Please use me or send someone to witness to them so that they can be saved.

Father, thank You for delivering me and giving me peace.

In Jesus' name I pray. Amen.

Scripture References

Romans 8:37	Psalm 27:3
2 Samuel 22:2	Isaiah 41:11-13
2 Samuel 22:4	Psalm 37:1-7,12,13
Psalm 55:18	Deuteronomy 28:7
Isaiah 54:4	Philippians 1:28

— 39 —

PEER PRESSURE

Father, please help me to be strong and not to give in to negative peer pressure. If the world is in darkness, and I am in the light, then no amount of their darkness can put out my light. I know that You will always provide a way out for me to keep from sin. I resist the lust and craving of my flesh and strive for integrity, faith, love, peace, and holiness in all of my relationships.

I know that You love me and want the best for me. I believe the things You warned me not to do in the Bible are not there to keep me from having fun, but to warn me of the dangers of sin. Sin thrills and then it kills; it fascinates and then it assassinates. So I won't follow the crowd to do evil, no matter how much they try to make me. I'll follow those who are godly examples, and I'll be a godly example for others. My security and self-esteem are in You. I don't need the approval of sinners to feel secure.

Father, I believe that You are making me into the person that You want me to be. Help me to become the strong witness that You want me to be — a bright light for the world, energized by faith in Your Word of life. Following You gives me happiness forever, not just an occasional good time.

I'm glad Jesus didn't give in to the temptations He faced. Your Word says that He was faced with every type of temptation there is, and still He didn't sin. Your Word also promises that Jesus is praying for me that my faith won't fail, so I won't give in either. I'll turn the tables on the devil by putting positive peer pressure on those who are pressuring me. I can pressure them to come to church and get saved.

My spirit, body, and soul belong to You, Father. I won't abuse Your property by sinning. I will avoid those who drink and smoke. Sin always leads to terrible pain. By Your grace I can endure all temptations. I can do all things through Jesus. Thank You for giving me wise words to silence my peers when they put pressure on me to sin. I won't compromise or bend to the right or to the left, but I'll keep my eyes straight ahead on Your Word.

I thank You that I'll be blessed for enduring temptations. When it's all over, I'll be a better, stronger person. Thank You for granting me wisdom in facing peer pressure and for giving me the foresight that I may avoid any unholy situations. I'll not follow in the ways that lead me into temptation, but I'll pursue and make only good, healthy relationships.

Thank You that in godliness I am blessed. I declare that I am strong and walk in wisdom today.

In Jesus' name I pray. Amen.

Scripture References

Psalm 27:1	1 Thessalonians 4:4
1 Corinthians 10:13	Hebrews 11:30
2 Timothy 2:22	Hebrews 4:15
John 3:16	Luke 22:32
Romans 6:23	2 Corinthians 6:16
1 Timothy 4:12	Philippians 4:13

— 40 —

FORGIVENESS WHEN YOU SIN

Father, I am sorry that I have sinned against You. You look at my heart, so I know that there is no way I can cover this sin myself. I don't deceive myself by trying to say that I have not sinned or by trying to hide it. There isn't anything that I can keep secret from You, because You know everything.

I know that there is a pleasure in sin for a season but that ultimately sin thrills and then it kills; it fascinates and then it assassinates. You have said that the wages of sin are death, but that if I confess my sins, You are faithful and just to forgive me of my sins and to cleanse me from all that is evil or not right.

I know that I'm not supposed to sin, and I confess right now that I have willingly and purposefully broken Your commandment and sinned. I knew better than to do that.

I believe that You are compassionate, slow to anger, and filled with mercy and love, so I run right to You when I sin and not away from You. So right now I confess _____ as sin. But I believe that I receive Your forgiveness and cleansing for my sins.

Father, I repent and ask You to help me never to do that again. I determine with Your help to make the necessary changes in my life and in my relationships with You and other people so that I will not commit this sin against You again.

Thank You for forgiving me and for giving me a pure heart and renewing a right spirit within me. I am blessed because You have canceled, forgiven, and forgotten all of my sins. You have removed the weight of sin and lifted the burden of guilt that has been weighing upon me. So by faith I believe that I am forgiven right now. I am not moved by what I feel; forgiveness is not a feeling. I am moved only by Your Word, which says that I am forgiven right now. So even if I don't feel forgiven right away, as I act holy and forgiven, the feelings will come.

So sin is not in control of my life any more. You are in control of my life. I am dead to sin, because I was crucified with Christ Jesus.

Father, I know that You and Jesus hate sin and that You love righteousness, and so I thank You for my forgiveness right now and that my fellowship and right relationship with You have been restored.

In Jesus' name I pray. Amen.

Scripture References

Psalm 103:2-4,8,11-13 AMP	Psalm 51:10
Hebrews 4:16	Psalm 32:1
1 John 1:10	Romans 6:13,14
Proverbs 28:13	Philippians 2:5,13
1 John 1:9	Hebrews 1:9

— 41 —

PORNOGRAPHY — SEXUAL SIN*

Father, I'm sorry for lusting or committing sexual sins with my body. I thank You that Your Word says that if I repent and confess my sin, You will always forgive me and cleanse me from all sin. I want to stay clean and pure. Help me not to give in to these urges I have in my body.

I present my body to You, consecrated to do Your will today, dedicated to live a holy life today. With Your help I determine to replace unclean movies or magazines or thoughts with the Word of God, that I might feed my spirit and develop into the righteous, victorious man/woman that You want me to be. I'd rather fellowship with the Holy Spirit through Your Word than with the unclean things of this world. When those thoughts try to take root in my mind, like a weed in a garden, I'll pluck them out by speaking Your Word with my mouth. As those pictures flash across my mind, like a TV screen, I'll simply change the channel by speaking Your Word.

Lord, help me to think and act like a holy, pure, righteous man/woman of God would. Teach me to possess my body in purity and honor. Help me to practice yielding my mind and my body to You as instruments of righteousness. Although it seems to be hard or impossible, I

---

*See prayer for "Forgiveness When You Sin."

know that nothing is impossible to those who believe.

Although these thought patterns and strongholds seem to be like a mountain, Your Word says that I can cast it into the ocean. So I declare, "Sin will no longer have dominion over me. I am more than a conqueror through Christ. I think and act like a righteous, victorious man/woman of God. My morals are strong, my purity is strong. Greater is He Who is in me than he who is in the world. I am of a royal priesthood, a holy nation, a chosen people. I'll think and act in this manner. I make a contract with my eyes not to lust after the opposite sex."

Body and mind, you listen to me. My spirit is in control now. You'll no longer think those thoughts or do those acts. You will yield to holiness instead of uncleanliness. When I say "Shut up," I mean *now*. When I say "No," I mean absolutely not. I will throw away all pornography and anything that is causing me to stumble.

I thank You for separating me away from such behavior through and through, so I can be sound, blameless, and spotless — in spirit, soul, and body. Help me to get out of any relationship that is dragging me down.

Lord, I'm making a decision to follow after You. I thank You for always making a way for me to keep from sinning. I'll keep myself pure for my spouse. You created me with sexual desires that are healthy, and I thank You that You've given me the grace to control those sexual desires until marriage.

Thank You, Father, that by faith I am free from sexual sin/pornography.

In Jesus' name I pray. Amen.

Scripture References

1 John 1:9	Luke 4:4
Romans 12:1,2	1 Thessalonians 4:4
1 Peter 1:18,19	Mark 11:23
2 Corinthians 10:3-5	Romans 6:13,14
Philippians 4:7,8	Romans 8:37
Job 31:1	1 John 4:4
Psalm 119:9	1 Peter 2:9
Hebrews 12:5,6	1 Corinthians 9:27
James 1:22	1 Thessalonians 5:23
Romans 8:5,6	Hebrews 4:16
1 Corinthians 10:13	

ALCOHOL — DRUG — CIGARETTE ADDICTION

Father, in the mighty name of Jesus, I come boldly to Your throne of grace that I may obtain mercy and find help in my time of need. I believe that You can deliver me and protect me from every evil.

Lord, I want to be free from alcohol/drugs, but I can't do it alone; I need Your help. I believe Your Word, and that truth will set me free, because if Jesus has made me free, I am free indeed. I need Your help to overcome temptation. Your Word says that being drunk or under the influence of liquor or drugs is a work of the flesh. So help me to walk in the Spirit, so I won't fulfill the lusts of the flesh. Help me to control my body with my spirit and mind, and make it obey Your Word.

Father, You are faithful because You will not allow me to be tempted beyond my powers of endurance. In every temptation You always show me a way out of it, so that I may be able to endure. I determine that I won't go to the wrong types of parties or places that will make it easier to give in to alcohol/drugs/cigarettes. I won't even associate with people who drink and use drugs. I still love these people, but I just can't be around them right now. Thank You for giving me friends who love You and desire to do Your will.

I will renew my mind by reading Your Word so that I can change the way I think and be set free from the habits and the lies that I have been believing. I believe that You can even change my desires, Father. Instead of alcohol/drugs/cigarettes, help me to desire, crave, and be addicted to Your Word and Your truth. Although it may seem impossible for me to quit, nothing is impossible with You, and to You this is a small thing. Nothing is too hard for You to accomplish.

Thank You that I have been freed from my sin by the blood of Jesus. Thank You for forgiving me and forgetting the sins of my past. I look to You to help me with a great, new future. It's a new day! Those sins are as far from me as the east is from the west. I am now a new person because of Jesus. All of my past life is dead and gone; I am a new creation.

Thank You, Father, for saving me from the hurt and destruction that sin causes. I yield my body to You. I resist sin and the devil, and they must flee from me.

Thank You, Lord, for a life free to serve You. Faith calls those things that be not as though they were, so by faith I call myself free right now. I'm not moved by how I feel; I'm moved only by what I believe. Your Word says I am free, so I am free indeed. I act free by taking my alcohol/drugs/cigarettes and throwing them away. I know that cigarette smoking won't send me to hell, but it will sure make me smell like I've been there; and alcohol preserves the dead and kills the living.

Father, I believe that I will never have to touch them again. Please lead and guide me to a good counselor or support group if that is what I need. Thank You that You are giving me good habits where I once had bad habits.

In Jesus' name I pray. Amen.

Scripture References

John 6:37

2 Timothy 4:18

2 Peter 2:9

1 Corinthians 10:13

Philippians 1:10

Ephesians 5:18

Galatians 5:18-21

1 Corinthians 9:27

1 Corinthians 15:33,34

Romans 13:14

1 Corinthians 10:13 Phillips

1 Corinthians 15:3 Beck

1 Corinthians 5:11

Psalm 37:4

Philippians 3:13

Psalm 103:11

2 Corinthians 5:17

Colossians 3:3

Romans 6:23

Philippians 4:8

James 4:7

WHEN YOU LOSE SOMETHING

Father, because I am Your child, I come boldly to Your throne of grace in my time of need. I ask in the mighty name of Jesus that You help me to find _____.

You are faithful to those who put their hope in You. Thank You that You care about even the smallest details in my life. You know exactly how many hairs I have on my head. I ask now that You will uncover what is hidden, because You know exactly where my _____ is. Your Word says that You know everything and that You are everywhere at the same time. I look to the Holy Spirit to show me where it is.

Holy Spirit, You know exactly where my _____ is. Please lead me to it. I commit the care of it unto You. I trust in You with all my heart. I look to You to reveal to me its whereabouts and I refuse to rely upon my own thoughts to find it.

Because You are Lord over all of my life, Father, You will straighten my course and watch my feet. If someone stole it, I forgive that person and pray that you will not let him or her sleep until he/she returns it to me. If someone happened to find it, please lead that individual to me or to someone I know.

Thank You, Lord, that the Holy Spirit will help me to remember where I last had it and that even the smallest details of its loss will come back to me. I ask my angels right now to go forth and help me find what I'm looking for. Nothing that is hidden can be kept in secret. You give me wisdom, knowledge, and understanding. Faith calls those things that be not as though they were, so by faith I say that I will find it very soon.

Thank You, Father, for guiding me and providing me with the answer. I give You all the glory. I will not talk doubt or unbelief concerning this thing, but my glad confession is that it is found. I have it now.

In Jesus' name I pray. Amen.

Scripture References

Proverbs 16:3	John 14:26
Lamentations 3:25	Isaiah 30:21 NIV
Luke 12:6,7	Matthew 10:26
Luke 8:17	Proverbs 2:6,7
James 1:5	Psalm 37:23
1 Corinthians 2:10	Psalm 73:24
Proverbs 3:5,6,7	

— 44 —

WHEN SOMEONE LIES ABOUT YOU

Father, I know that the devil is a liar and the father of lies. Your Word says that all liars will have their place in the lake that burns with fire. So I pray for _____ who has lied about me. Please open his/her eyes so that he/she may see and understand the truth so that he/she can be delivered from this darkness he/she is in.

Your Word says that I am supposed to pray for those who persecute me and that I am to love my enemies, so I pray for _____ and choose to forgive him/her as You have forgiven me. People lied about Jesus too, so it shouldn't surprise me that they lie about me.

I know that the truth always wins over a lie in the long run. You see everything and You know what has happened, so I don't have to worry or be afraid.

Thank You, Father, that You will deliver me and help me not to be ashamed. As I trust in You and continue to walk in honesty, integrity, and pureness of heart, I will keep Your Word before me, so that a root of bitterness may not develop in my heart. My anger does not accomplish Your will. Vengeance is Yours, Lord, so I will not strike back in revenge and I will not fight a lie with a lie, but I will fight the fiery lies of the devil with the water of Your Word — and Your Word will quench that fire.

I ask that You help protect me from these lies, and I'll trust and wait patiently for You. As people see that I'm not nervous or striking back, they will recognize the truth. Help me not to worry or be angry about what has happened. I believe that You'll make the truth in this situation obvious to everyone involved, and that the hidden things will be brought to the light.

Father, I ask that if _____ is not saved, You will send someone to him/her who can share Jesus with him/her. I pray that You will make it possible for _____ to know Your Son, Jesus, as his/her personal Savior.

Thank You for putting a guard on my lips to help me to watch what I say, so that I do not fall into the sin of lying. I do not want to say anything at all that will not build others up. Please help me to learn to be quick to hear, slow to speak, and slow to anger. I will not let the devil steal my joy through this lie. So by faith I'll have a song in my heart, a spring in my step, and a smile on my lips.

I thank You, Father, that You always cause me to triumph in Christ Jesus and that you've given me favor like a shield with all those who are involved.

In Jesus' name I pray. Amen.

Scripture References

John 8:44	Psalm 37:6-8,3
Ephesians 1:18	NIV, KJV
Matthew 5:44	Proverbs 21:23
Matthew 6:14,15	Ephesians 4:29
Psalm 37:1	James 1:19
Psalm 101:6,7	Psalm 25:20,21
Matthew 9:28	Psalm 26:1
	Psalm 119:23

— 45 —

WHEN OTHERS MAKE FUN OF YOU

Father, I come to You in the name that is above all other names — the name of Jesus. You hold me in the palm of Your hand and Your name is a strong tower that I can run into and be safe even when people make fun of me. I try to smile and just ignore what they are saying, but deep down it really hurts.

I want to be accepted by others, but I have to follow You first. I know that Jesus was tempted just as I am, but He didn't give in to sin or hate. Please give me Your mercy and grace to deal with this situation. I look to You for my comfort; You are a true friend any time I need one.

Thank You for never leaving me alone or rejecting me. I know that it must have hurt Jesus when people made fun of and mocked Him. There were times when even the people closest to Him thought He was crazy. I'm thankful that He did not quit in the middle of what You wanted Him to do, Father. Help me to have that same strength.

By faith, I forgive the people who have made fun of me. Specifically right now I forgive _____. Please open his/her eyes to see how cutting his/her words are.

Father, please use me or send other Christians to witness to him/her about Jesus. I won't be mean or resentful towards him/her, and I will not give in to the temptation to make fun of him/her or to strike back in anger. I will love him/her with the love of Jesus in me, and Your love will lead him/her to repent and be saved.

Thank You for Your patience, compassion, and love in me. I will not be easily offended. I'll believe only the truth about myself, not the lies that some people tell. Thank You for sending and giving me friends who will stand by me during this time.

Your Word says I can do all things because Jesus lives in me. I'm going to keep doing right, and speaking good things, and living for You. I am not ashamed of the Gospel, and because You're not ashamed of me, I'm not ashamed of myself. If people make fun of me because of my relationship with Jesus, or for any other reason, it won't bother me because Your Word says that I'm the one who will be happy and blessed in the end.

So by faith I declare that in the midst of all these things I am more than a conqueror through Jesus Who loves me. You always cause me to triumph and win because of Him.

In Jesus' name I pray. Amen.

Scripture References

Hebrews 4:15	1 John 3:13
1 Corinthians 10:13	1 Corinthians 4:4
Proverbs 18:24	1 John 4:4
2 Timothy 2:13	Romans 8:37
1 John 3:13	Colossians 2:15
Ephesians 4:32	Philippians 4:13
Matthew 6:14,15	Romans 1:16
Romans 5:5	Matthew 5:10-12
Colossians 1:10,11	Psalm 1:1
Psalm 119:165	

— 46 —

WHEN YOU FEEL LONELY OR UNLOVED

Father, when other people leave me and I feel unloved, I am thankful that You will never, ever leave me alone or reject me. You are a help for me in this time of trouble. I know Your angels are all around me.

There is a report in Your Word about David, a man who was a hero one minute and the next minute all of his friends wanted to kill him. David didn't feel sorry for himself, but Your Word says that David encouraged himself in You, Lord. So I encourage myself in You also. You are my God. I know that You love me.

Jesus even gave His life for me. I'm a born-again Christian. Jesus lives in my heart, and I'm on my way to heaven. That is plenty to be thankful for. So I won't allow myself to be discouraged or feel sorry for myself. I choose to think only on those things that are pure, and holy, and good, even when I'm alone.

Heavenly Father, I trust You to strengthen me and help me right now. Although I may feel alone, thank You that my life is not ruled by feelings. I know that I am not alone, for Your Word says that there is nothing that can separate me from the love of Christ — not pain, or stress, or persecution. I will come out on top of every circumstance or trial through Jesus' love.

131

So I submit myself to You and resist the devil, in the name of Jesus, and he must flee from me. He has to pack up his loneliness, discouragement, and self-pity and go from me right now. I refuse to think on the devil's thoughts of loneliness any longer.

I command my feelings to come in line with the Word of God. I will not be bitter or resentful to those who are unfriendly. I'm going to follow Jesus' example. When all His disciples and friends left Him, He said, "I am not alone, because the Father is with me." (John 16:32.) You love me and have told me to love even those who are mean to me. So I pray right now and forgive those who may have treated me badly and I ask that Your love will become a reality to them.

Father, I thank You that You give me all the desires of my heart when I am following after You. It is a desire of my heart to have Christian friends who love You. Help me to walk in Your love that You put in my heart. I know that there are a lot of lonely people in the world You want to reach out to. Use me to touch them with Your love as I show myself friendly to them. And as I take my eyes off myself, I know that those feelings of loneliness will disappear.

I have so much to be thankful for, Father. Thank You that Jesus is a friend Who sticks closer than a brother.

In Jesus' name I pray. Amen.

Scripture References

Hebrews 13:5,6	Romans 8:37
Deuteronomy 31:8	Ephesians 4:31,32
1 Samuel 30:6	Luke 6:27,28
John 3:16	Psalm 37:4
Romans 10:9,10	Romans 5:5
John 14:1-3	Ephesians 5:1,2
Philippians 4:8	Romans 12:21
Romans 8:35	John 16:32

— 47 —

A BROKEN HOME

Father, Your Word says that when my mom or my dad leaves me, You will help me and hold me up in the palm of Your hand, because I am the apple of Your eye. I need Your help right now. I get frustrated sometimes thinking about what has happened to my parents and family, but I look to You as my help. You can mend our hurts and heal our broken hearts. Jesus said that He would never leave us comfortless or without help, so thank You that Your Holy Spirit is here now to comfort us.

Help me by Your Holy Spirit to be strong. I will not allow myself to become bitter or to speak bad or evil words about anyone, even though I may feel like it. I am kind, loving, and forgiving, just like Jesus. I am going to think only on the things that are good, pure, true, clean, and holy. If I am angry, I will not sin. I'll continue to look to You for help rather than opening the door for the devil to harm me.

Jesus said that His peace is different from any earthly or human peace. So, Father, I ask for that kind of supernatural peace to keep me from being worried or afraid. Thank You for giving me and my family a peace that is more wonderful than anyone can imagine.

I don't understand all that is going on with my family, so I pray that You will show my parents and family the right decisions to make. I pray that they will realize the love that You have for them and that You will be their friend also.

Show the unsaved members of my family that they need to ask Jesus to be their Savior. And send someone across their path from whom they can receive counsel, and help them to forgive each other so there will be a healing in their relationship.

Father, although this situation seems hopeless, there is nothing that is impossible for You. You sent Jesus so that we could have life to the fullest, but the devil is trying to steal, kill, and destroy our family. So by faith, with the authority of Jesus' name, I bind Satan and command him to take his hands off every member of my family.

I know that each person has his or her own will and can choose to follow You or reject You, Father. Although I really love all my family, I will not allow them to drag me down into depression, discouragement, despair, hatred, or strife, because Your joy is my strength. The devil may try to lie to me and tell me that these family problems are my fault, but I know that he is a liar and the father of lies, so I cast down those thoughts and imaginations and I won't think about them.

The truth is that the works of the devil and the works of the flesh are to blame — things like selfishness, anger, lust, hatred, and pride. So I pray and ask that the fruit of the Spirit — love, joy, peace, humility, meekness, and self-control — will replace these evil works. Thank You that I can be a light and a hope for my family.

Father, thank You for moving in my family and protecting all of us from harm or evil. By faith, I say that it is a new day and that You are doing a new thing in my family.

In Jesus' name I pray. Amen.

Scripture References

Psalm 27:10	Philippians 4:6,7
Psalm 147:3	Proverbs 3:5,6
Ephesians 4:31,32	Ephesians 3:14-19
Philippians 4:8	Acts 16:31
Ephesians 4:26,27	Galatians 5:19-23
John 14:27	

PHYSICALLY, SEXUALLY, OR VERBALLY ABUSED*

Father, thank You that I can run to You for safety and protection and that You are my shield from evil or harm. I am the apple of Your eye and You hold me in the palm of Your hand.

Lord, You have said that in Jesus' name I have authority over all evil and darkness. In Psalm 91 You say that I can trample on top of all demons and evil. So I command Satan and his demons who are motivating this person to hurt me, to take his/her hands off God's property.

Father, You say that no plague or evil will come near my house, so I don't have to put up with this in the name of Jesus.

The devil has tried to lie to me and tell me that I deserve this or that I brought this upon myself, but I reject that thought and cast it down in the mighty name of Jesus. It is the devil and the works of the flesh, like greed, lust, hatred, pride, and selfishness, that have influenced this person's actions. But I will demonstrate the fruit of the Spirit which is love, joy, peace, meekness, humility, and self-control.

I know that the weapons of my warfare are not worldly, but they are much more powerful than the weapons of devils and I can pull down strongholds with them. So I use Your Word as

*See "Protection."

a powerful weapon against this evil. I cast down any evil thought or imagination. In the name of Jesus I bring into captivity every thought to the obedience of Christ.

I thank You that no weapon formed against me will succeed. Thank You that You will make my enemies to be at peace with me.

Father, You said that when I feel rejection from people, I should know that You still love me because You'll never leave me alone or reject me. I know that in order for faith to work, I have to forgive. So I forgive _____ right now.

You said that I should pray for those who come against me and do evil against me, so I pray for _____ right now. I know it is the devil who has influenced his/her actions. I pray that You will open this person's eyes and heal him/her. I thank You that Jesus died for this person's sins just as He died for mine. I thank You that You will send laborers across _____'s path so they can minister to him/her and deliver him/her from this evil behavior.

So, Father, now that I have forgiven _____ and I have a pure heart, I know that You have said that those things which are done in secret will be brought to the light and the hidden things will be brought into the open. So show me who I should tell this to, so that _____ can no longer be allowed to do this to me or anyone else. Prepare the heart of that person so that I can go to my parents, teachers, pastor, the police, or someone who can make sure that this doesn't happen anymore —

someone who will keep _____ from doing this to me.

Help me to keep Your joy and help me not to be bitter. I will not allow any feelings of bitterness, hate, resentment, or evil to live in my heart. I release these feelings in Jesus' name. I resist rejection and lies. I tell them that they have to go in Jesus' name. I take these thoughts captive and bring them into the obedience of Christ. I replace them with Your Word, Father, which says that I am righteous, holy, pure, and good in Your eyes. I will think on things that are true, clean, right, pure, and holy, so I will meditate in Your Word day and night.

Your Word says that the battle is in the spirit, not against other people. And I thank You that You have already won the victory for me through Jesus Who bought me with a price. My body is the temple of the Holy Ghost so I will not let anyone treat it any differently. Satan must pay back seven times what he has stolen from me. So I claim a sevenfold return of love, acceptance, and security that has been taken from my life.

I thank You for healing my broken heart, bandaging my wounds and healing my mind and emotions. Jesus died so that I can be healed of these pains. You are holding my hand and saying, "Don't be afraid, I will help you." I pray that You will bring back the good of these years. I trust in You for You are a mighty God. By faith I say that it is a new day in my life and my future years will be better than my past.

Father, You are my source of justice and I determine that I won't act out of revenge, but I will let You choose the instrument — whether the police, my family, or someone else — to minister Your justice and judgment.

Thank You for protecting me from evil and harm, and for purifying me and cleansing my heart. What the devil has meant for harm, I know that You can turn for good. I will not be afraid, for I know that You are stronger than the devil. And Jesus, Who is in me, is greater than he who is in the world.

I'm going on with my life; I won't let what other people do or say drag me down. Please help me find wise and godly people who can listen, counsel, and minister to me so that I can get over this quickly. I thank You that You have a plan for my life, and I will be able to fulfill that plan.

In Jesus' name I pray. Amen.

Scripture References

2 Samuel 22:3	James 4:7
1 Peter 2:24	2 Corinthians 10:5
Luke 4:18	2 Corinthians 5:21
Romans 5:19	Isaiah 40:8
John 3:16	Philippians 4:8
Hebrews 13:5	2 Corinthians 10:3-5
Matthew 6:14	Matthew 18:18
Matthew 5:44	Proverbs 6:30,31
Revelation 12:10	Psalm 147:3,6
Proverbs 16:7	Isaiah 41:13
Ephesians 1:16	Jeremiah 30:17
Nehemiah 8:10	Joel 2:25
Hebrews 12:15	

— 49 —

BOYFRIEND/GIRLFRIEND BREAKS UP

Father, I pour my heart out to You about my boyfriend/girlfriend. You are my strength, and my help comes from You whenever I am hurt or in trouble. Thank You that You are the God of all comfort, so I ask You to encourage me today. I thank You that You will strengthen my heart with Your power by Your Holy Spirit.

I commit my dating life to You, and I believe that You will help me to get through this because I am trusting in You. Your Word says that it is better for me to trust in You than to put my confidence in other people because people can let me down. But You will never let me down, and You'll never leave me, forsake me, or reject me.

I believe that You are working things out and comforting me even now. I may be sad, but I'm not giving up hope. Teach me to guard my heart with all diligence. Grant me wisdom and instruct me in my social life that I may grow in this area. My joy comes from You anyway, Father, and the joy of the Lord is my strength.

Jesus, thank You for making Yourself more real to me than ever, so I can be strong in Your love, the love that passes all human understanding. Your love, not dating relationships, gives me security and peace. I ask that You give _____ your peace, too.

Even though I don't totally understand why we broke up, Father, I still want Your best for him/her. Thank You for healing his/her broken heart and for sending laborers across his/her path to encourage and comfort him/her. In the name of Jesus I take authority over any spirit of rejection, loneliness, depression, or suicide that would try to cause either of us to do something stupid. Help both of us to get on with our lives.

Help me not to speak any evil words of hate or bitterness over this relationship in the name of Jesus. I thank You that You can use this situation for good so that when others are going through this same thing, I may be able to help and encourage them.

Thank You, Father, that Your Spirit is doing a healing work on my broken heart, and that I can be strong spiritually and emotionally, and that this will be a quick recovery. I won't be worried, nervous, or act in fear, because I know that You have someone else for me to date. I determine to be content and patient until that opportunity arises. Thank You that You hold me in the palm of Your hand and that You are always working on my behalf.

In Jesus' name I pray. Amen.

Scripture References

Psalm 62:8	Ephesians 1:17
Hebrews 13:16	Hebrews 12:15
2 Timothy 1:12	Psalm 37:4
Psalm 118:8	Ephesians 3:20
Romans 8:28	2 Corinthians 1:3
Psalm 73:26	Proverbs 4:20
Nehemiah 8:10	Ephesians 3:16
Ephesians 3:18,19	

Other Books
by Word Ministries, Inc.

A Call To Prayer

Prayers That Avail Much — Volume I

Prayers That Avail Much — Volume II

Prayers That Avail Much — Spanish Edition

Prayers That Avail Much — Special Edition

Prayers That Avail Much for Mothers

Prayers That Avail Much for Fathers

Also on Prayer
From Little Castle Books

Prayers That Avail Much for Children
by Angela Brown

Prayers That Avail Much for Children
Book 2

**Available from your local bookstore,
or by writing:**

HARRISON HOUSE
P.O. Box 35035 • Tulsa, OK 74153

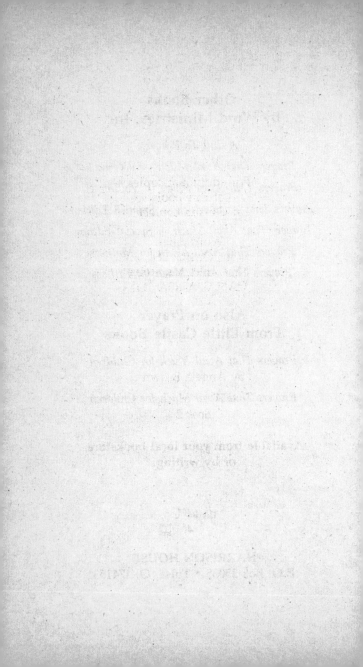

For additional copies
of this book
in Canada contact:

Word Alive
P. O. Box 284
Niverville, Manitoba
CANADA R0A 1E0

The Harrison House Vision

Proclaiming the truth and the power
Of the Gospel of Jesus Christ
With excellence;

Challenging Christians to
Live victoriously,
Grow spiritually,
Know God Intimately.